D1232936

TALK TO ME IN KOREAN

LEVEL 7

Tell Stories, Express Ideas, and
Hold Deeper Conversations

This book is based on a series of published lessons,
divided into ten levels, which are currently available
at TalkToMeInKorean.com.

대릉원

TALK TO ME IN KOREAN
- LEVEL 7 -

Talk To Me In Korean - Level 7

| 1판 1쇄 | 1st edition published | 2019. 09. 16 |
| 1판 2쇄 | 2nd edition published | 2020. 05. 12 |

지은이	Written by	TalkToMeInKorean
책임편집	Edited by	선경화 Kyung-hwa Sun, 에밀리 프리즈러키 Emily Przylucki
디자인	Designed by	선윤아 Yoona Sun
삽화	Illustrations by	김경해 Kyounghae Kim
녹음	Voice Recordings by	선현우 Hyunwoo Sun, 최경은 Kyeong-eun Choi
펴낸곳	Published by	롱테일북스 Longtail Books
펴낸이	Publisher	이수영 Su Young Lee
편집	Copy-edited by	김보경 Florence Kim
주소	Address	04043 서울 마포구 양화로 12길 16-9(서교동) 북앤빌딩 3층
		3rd Floor Book-And Bldg. 16-9 Yanghwa-ro 12-gil, Mapo-gu, Seoul, KOREA
이메일	E-mail	TTMIK@longtailbooks.co.kr
ISBN		979-11-86701-98-0 14710

이 도서의 국립중앙도서관 출판예정도서목록(CIP)은 서지정보유통지원시스템 홈페이지(http://seoji.nl.go.kr)와
국가자료종합목록 구축시스템(http://kolis-net.nl.go.kr)에서 이용하실 수 있습니다.
(CIP제어번호 : CIP2019034322)

TTMIK - TALK TO ME IN KOREAN

MESSAGE
FROM
THE AUTHOR

Congratulations on reaching Level 7! At this level, you already know how to form and understand complex sentences in Korean as well as express the same idea in various ways. After studying with this textbook, you will be able to use even more useful sentence endings to say things with greater accuracy and deliver your messages and feelings more clearly.

Knowing one more sentence ending or grammar point, however, does not automatically make you more fluent. The easiest way to make sure you remember what you have learned is to use it in real-life situations. If you can talk to native speakers, that is great! If you cannot, there are many other ways you can practice speaking with someone in Korean, such as through social media or language exchange services. Whichever method you choose, please continue practicing at least a little bit every day!

You are now one TTMIK textbook closer to your desired fluency level. We hope you continue enjoying our curriculum. 이번 책도 많은 도움이 되었으면 좋겠습니다! 앞으로도 재미있게 한국어 공부하세요!

TABLE OF CONTENTS

LESSON 1

I see that…, I just realized that…

-(는)구나/군요

Track 01

In this lesson, we are looking at the sentence endings -(는)구나 and -(는)군요. -(는)구나 is used in 반말 (casual, informal language) while -(는)군요 is only used in 존댓말 (polite, formal language).

When are they used?

You can use -(는)구나 and -(는)군요 when you just realized or found out about something for the first time, mainly to express your realization. You can sometimes use these endings to show that you are surprised, but this depends on the intonation of your sentence.

Let us compare some sentences using -(는)구나 or -(는)군요 endings with some plain sentences.

I. 여기 있었어요. = It was here.
(존댓말) 여기 있었군요. = (I see that) It was here.
(반말) 여기 있었구나. (same meaning as above)

2. 생각보다 비싸요. = It is more expensive than I thought.

(존댓말) 생각보다 비싸군요. = (I see that) It is more expensive than I thought.

(반말) 생각보다 비싸구나. (same meaning as above)

3. 여기 살아요. = I live here. / She lives here. / They live here.

(존댓말) 여기 사는군요. = (I see that) You live here.

(반말) 여기 사는구나. = (same meaning as above)

> ### *Conjugation*
>
> Past Tense:
> Verb stem + -았/었/였군요
> Verb stem + -았/었/였구나
>
> Present Tense:
> - Action Verbs: Verb stem + -는군요/는구나
> - Descriptive Verbs (Adjectives in infinitive form): Verb stem + -군요/구나

Track
01

-(는)군요 and -(는)군

Generally, when you drop the -요 at the end of a Korean sentence, it becomes a 반말 sentence; it is the same with -(는)군요. If you say -(는)군, it has the same level as -(는)구나. Even though the basic meaning is the same, however, -(는)구나 is more commonly used in spoken language and sounds happier than -(는)군. Sometimes people will say -(는)군, but it will make your sentence sound a bit like written language and more serious.

Ex)

이거 맛있구나.

= (I did not know before but I just realized that) This is delicious!

이거 맛있군.

→ This sentence has the same basic meaning as the one above, but it sounds a little more masculine and more like written language.

Some might be wondering what is the difference between -구나 and -네. The difference is if you say, "맛있네", you are asking for the other person's opinion as well.

Nouns + -군요/구나

If you want to use a noun, you can use the form "Noun + -이다". If the noun ends with a consonant, you keep the -이 and add -군요 or -구나.

Ex) 학생이군요. / 학생이구나.

If the noun ends with a vowel, you drop the -이 and just add -군요 or -구나.

Ex) 이거군요. / 이거구나.

Sample Sentences

여기 진짜 넓구나!

= This place is so big!

* If you just say, "여기 진짜 넓어요!", it is not as natural since you are trying to show that you are surprised.

이게 그거였군요!

= So this was about what you were talking!

이 사람 그 사람이었구나.

= This was that person about whom you were talking.

이렇게 하는 거군요.

= So this is how you do it!

벌써 11월이구나!

= (I did not realize before but) It is already November!

어제도 만났군요.

= (I did not know before but I just found out that) You met yesterday too.

Track 01

Sample Dialogue

Track
02

민경: 이 신발 누구 거예요? 진짜 귀엽다.

현주: 주연이 신발이에요.

민경: 와! 주연이 발이 진짜 작군요.

현주: 네. 주연이가 키에 비해서 발이
　　　작은 편이에요.

민경: 아, 그렇군요.

Minkyung: Whose shoes are these? They are so cute.

Hyunjoo: They are Jooyeon's shoes.

Minkyung: Wow! (I didn't know before but I just realized
　　　that) Jooyeon's feet are very small!

Hyunjoo: Yes. Jooyeon's feet are relatively small compared
　　　to her height.

Minkyung: Oh, I see.

Tell Stories, Express Ideas, and

✎ Exercises for Lesson 1

Change the ending of the plain sentences below by using -(는)구나 *or* -(는)군요 *so they can express your realization.*

Check the answers on **p.199**

1. 여기 있었어요.

(존댓말) ....

(반말) ....

2. 생각보다 비싸요.

(존댓말) ....

(반말) ....

3. 여기 살아요.

(존댓말) ....

(반말) ....

4. 이렇게 하는 거예요.

(존댓말) ....

(반말) ....

5. 이게 그거였어요.

(존댓말) ....

(반말) ....

LESSON 2

To pretend to + verb

-(으/느)ㄴ 척하다/체하다

Track 03

In this lesson, we will look at how to say "to pretend" to do something in Korean. The key words that you need to know are 척 and 체. Their usage is slightly different, but the basic form is:

Verb stem + -(으/느)ㄴ 척하다

or

Verb stem + -(으/느)ㄴ 체하다

In the structures above, both 체 and 척 have the meaning of "the act of pretending" or "acting as if". The part before 척/체, which is -(으/느)ㄴ, has the role of changing a verb into the adjective form, and the verb 하다 means "to do".

-(으/느)ㄴ = adjective ending

척/체 = the act of pretending   →   -(으/느)ㄴ 척하다/체하다

하다 = to do

Examples

(1)

알다 = to know

→ 아는 척하다 = to pretend to know

→ 아는 체하다 = to pretend to know

* Here, 알다 is a ㄹ irregular verb, so drop the ㄹ.

(2)

자다 = to sleep

→ 자는 척하다 = to pretend to sleep

→ 자는 체하다 = to pretend to sleep

(3)

Track 03

예쁘다 = to be pretty

→ 예쁜 척하다 = to pretend to be pretty, to act as if one was pretty

→ 예쁜 체하다 = to pretend to be pretty, to act as if one was pretty

You can use -(으/느)ㄴ 척하다/체하다 with past tense and present progressive, too.

Examples

(1)

알다 → 알고 있다 (present progressive)

→ 알고 있는 척하다/체하다 = to pretend to be aware of something

* 알다 literally means "to be knowing", but since this is not natural in English, you can translate it as "to be aware of".

(2)

자다 → 자고 있다 (present progressive)

→ 자고 있는 척하다/체하다 = to pretend to be sleeping/asleep

(3)

하다 → 한 (past tense adjective form)

→ 한 척하다/체하다 = to pretend to have done something

(4)

일하다 → 일하고 있다 (present progressive)

→ 일하고 있는 척하다/체하다 = to pretend to be working

(5)

먹다 → 먹은 (past tense adjective form)

→ 먹은 척하다/체하다 = to pretend to have eaten something

   * You cannot use -(으/느)ㄴ 척하다/체하다 with future tense. In that case you need to use different grammar structures, such as -(으)ㄹ 것처럼 행동하다, etc.

Difference Between 척 and 체

I. -(으/느)ㄴ 척 can be used as a stand-alone clause without the 하다 ending, whereas -(으/느)ㄴ 체 cannot.

   Ex)

   모르는 척, 조용히 나갔어요.

    = (While) Pretending as if they did not know, they went out quietly.

Here there is only the verb 모르다 and the structure -는 척 without 하다. 모르는 척 can be translated as "pretending as if they did not know", so 모르는 척 can be used here as a singular clause.

척 is used more in spoken language than 체, but there is no clear rule on this. Since people tend to use 척 more often, it tends to have a stronger nuance.

2. Only 척 can be followed by verbs other than 하다, which is usually 행동하다 (to behave) or 이야기하다 (to talk). However, even in those cases, those verbs are mostly "related" to the verb 하다.

For example, when you want to say, "Stop pretending you know" you can say, "아는 척하지 마세요" but also, "아는 척 그만하세요." Here, 그만하다 means to stop, but it basically comes from 하다.

Track 03

Sample Sentences

모르는 척하지 말고 빨리 말해 줘요.

= Please do not pretend you do not know and tell me quickly.

자는 척 그만하고 일어나요.

= Stop pretending to be asleep and get up.

공부한 척하지 마세요.

= Do not pretend that you studied.

공부 안 한 척하지 마세요.

= Do not pretend you did not study.

17

공부하는 척하지 마세요.

= 공부하고 있는 척하지 마세요.

= Do not pretend to be studying.

그 사람은 예쁜 척을 너무 많이 해요.

= She behaves (too much) as if she is pretty.

　　* 예쁜 척 often gets used as a noun.

아는 척하지 마세요.

= Do not pretend to know.

= Do not be a know-it-all.

　　* 아는 척 is the act of knowing everything. To be a know-it-all.

**Track
03**

Sample Dialogue

Track 04

캐시: 아까 왜 저 못 본 척했어요?

현우: 언제요?

캐시: 아까 복도에서 제가 인사했는데 못 본 척했잖아요.

현우: 아, 정말요? 아니에요. 진짜 못 봤어요. 죄송해요.

Cassie: Why did you pretend not to see me earlier?

Hyunwoo: When?

Cassie: A little while ago in the hall, I said hello, and you pretended you didn't see me, didn't you?

Hyunwoo: Oh, really? No way. I really didn't see you. I'm sorry.

✏ Exercises for Lesson 2

Translate the following phrases into Korean.

1. to pretend to know

....

2. to pretend to sleep

....

3. to pretend to be sleeping/asleep

....

4. to pretend to be pretty, to act as if one was pretty

....

Check the answers on **p.199**

5. to pretend to be working

....

LESSON 3

To be doable/understandable/bearable

-(으)ㄹ 만하다

In this lesson, we will look at the structure -(으)ㄹ 만하다. This structure has a variety of meanings so it is very important to pay close attention to the context in order to understand what is the intention.

Track 05

Generally, -(으)ㄹ 만하다 means that there is enough reason or justification for a certain situation, or that something is doable or possible, but mainly in the sense of being "bearable" to do.

Let us take a look at some examples.

가다
→ 갈 만하다
= to be possible to go
= to be worth going (and checking out the place)
= there is enough justifiable reason for one to go

21

Ex)

입장료 만 원이라서 갈 만해요.

= The entrance fee is just 10,000 won, so it is worth going.

* In this situation, it sounds like other places are much more expensive than 10,000 won, perhaps 50,000 won. So, your intention is more like, "Since this place is cheaper, it is worth going."

먹다

→ 먹을 만하다

= to be edible

= to taste okay (the taste is bearable)

= the taste is acceptable

Track 05

Ex)

먹을 만해요?

= Does it taste okay?

늦다

→ 늦을 만하다

= to be forgivable for being late

= there is enough reason for being late

놀라다

→ 놀랄 만하다

= to be natural to be surprised/shocked

= there is enough reason to be surprised/shocked

Sample Sentences

그럴 만해요.

= It is understandable to be so.

= It is possible.

= There is enough reason for it to be so.

    * This is a fixed phrase.

그 사람은 인기가 있을 만해요.

= There is enough reason that he is popular.

= It is understandable why he is popular.

이 책 읽을 만해요?

= Is this book worth reading?

= Is this book good?

= Do you recommend this book?

    * This sounds more natural than saying, "추천해요? (= Do you recommend it?)"

Track 05

괜찮아요. 참을 만해요.

= I am okay. It is endurable.

= I am okay. I can bear it.

가족끼리 한 번쯤 갈 만해요.

= (The place) is worth visiting once (or twice) with family.

Sample Dialogue

Track
06

승우: 요즘 볼 만한 드라마 없어요?

두나: 비밀의 숲이라는 드라마 알아요?

승우: 아니요. 그 드라마 재밌어요?

두나: 네, 진짜 재밌어요. 꼭 보세요. 정말
볼 만해요.

Seung-woo: Are there any good dramas these days?

Doona: Do you know the drama called Stranger?

Seung-woo: No. Is it good?

*Doona: Yes, it's really good. You should definitely
watch it. It's really worth watching.*

🖊 *Exercises for Lesson* **3**

Fill in the blanks by using -(으)ㄹ 만해요.

1. (   )

     = It is understandable to be so.

     = It is possible.

     = There is enough reason for it to be so.

2. 그 사람은 인기가 (   ).

     = There is enough reason that he is popular.

     = It is understandable why he is popular.

3. 이 책 (   ) ?

     = Is this book worth reading?

     = Is this book good?

     = Do you recommend this book?

4. 괜찮아요. (   ).

     = I am okay. It is endurable.

     = I am okay. I can bear it.

5. 가족끼리 한 번쯤 (   ).

     = (The place) is worth visiting once (or twice) with family.

Check the answers on **p.199**

LESSON 4

Like + noun

-같이, -처럼

Track 07

In this lesson, we will look at the words -같이 and -처럼. They are both particles (used after nouns) that mean "like + Noun". When you use -같이 or -처럼 after a word, the word group works more like an adverb in a sentence (i.e. "like a robot", "like a Korean girl", etc.).

Many people make the mistake of using -같이 and -처럼 with the verb "to be", but more on that later in this lesson.

Noun + -같이/처럼 = like + Noun, as + Noun

Examples

(1)
종이 + -처럼 = 종이처럼
= like paper
→ 종이처럼 가볍다 = to be light like paper
→ 종이같이 가볍다 = to be light like paper

(2)

로봇 + -처럼 = 로봇처럼

= like a robot

→ 로봇처럼 걷다 = to walk like a robot

→ 로봇같이 걷다 = to walk like a robot

Sample Sentences

저처럼 해 보세요.

= Try doing it like I do.

그 사람은 한국어를 한국 사람처럼 잘해요.

= He/She speaks Korean well like a Korean person.

제가 어제 말한 것처럼 했어요?

= Did you do it like I said yesterday?

Track 07

All of the sentences above can be written with -같이 in the place of -처럼.

→ 저같이 해 보세요.

→ 그 사람은 한국어를 한국 사람같이 잘해요.

→ 제가 어제 말한 것같이 했어요?

* -처럼 and -같이 are interchangeable in most cases, so whichever sounds more natural depends on the person's opinion.

같이 and -같이

Even though they are basically the same word, there is a difference in the meaning between using -같이 after a noun and 같이 independently. When 같이 is used independently as an adverb, it means "together". In this case, you would often need the particle -와 or -(이)랑 which means "with".

Ex)
저 사람같이 하세요
= Do like that person does.

저 사람이랑 같이 하세요.
= Do it together with that person.

Track 07

-같이 and 같은

When you add -같이 after a noun, it works as an adverb. When you want to make the expression work as an adjective, you can add 같은 instead of -같이. However, you have to put a space between the noun and 같은 unlike -같이, because 같은 is not a particle but a conjugated form of the adjective (aka. descriptive verb), 같다.

Ex)
저 같은 사람
= a person like me
= somebody like me

Sample Sentences

강아지가 곰처럼 생겼어요.

= The puppy looks like a bear.

오늘은 일요일 같은 월요일이에요.

= Today is a Monday (that feels) like a Sunday.

제 친구는 미국인인데 영어를 영국 사람처럼 해요.

= My friend is American but she/he speaks English like a British person.

바보처럼 정말 그 말을 믿었어요?

= Did you really believe that like a fool?

Track 07

Sample Dialogue

선미: 둘이 항상 같이 다녀요?

지은: 네. 저희는 가족 같은 사이예요.

선미: 둘이 나이 차이 많이 나지 않아요?

지은: 많이 나는데 저희는 친구처럼 지내요.

Seonmi: Are you two always together?

Ji-eun: Yes. We are like family.

Seonmi: Isn't there a big age gap between you two?

Ji-eun: There is, but we get on with each other like friends.

✎ Exercises for Lesson **4**

Complete each sentence by choosing either 같이 or 같은 to fill in the blank.

1. 저 (   ) 사람 처음 봤어요?

2. 저 사람이랑 (   ) 하세요.

3. 그 사람은 한국어를 한국 사람 (   ) 잘해요.

4. 바보 (   ) 정말 그 말을 믿었어요?

5. 오늘은 일요일 (   ) 월요일이에요.

Check the answers on **p.199**

LESSON 5

As much as

만큼

Track 09

In this lesson, we are going to take a look at how to use the word **만큼** to say things like, "He is as tall as I am" and, "You can take as much as you want" in Korean.

만큼 can be used both as a particle and as a noun. When it is used after other nouns, pronouns, and prepositions, it works as a particle; write it right after the previous word without a space. When it is used after a verb, it must be modified to work as a noun. Either way, the basic meaning is the same.

만큼 represents the meaning of "as much as" or "to the point of" doing or being something.

Examples

I.
저만큼
= 저 + 만큼
= as much as me

32

= as much as I

* This one depends on the intonation and could even mean "as much as that".

2.

이만큼

= 이(것) + 만큼

= as much as this

= this much

3.

놀랄 만큼

= 놀라다 + 만큼

= to the point of one being surprised

= surprisingly

* This one is written a bit differently as there is a space between 놀랄 and 만큼. This is because 만큼 is being used as a noun here.

4.

원하는 만큼

= 원하다 + 만큼

= as much as one wants

* You will notice that in 놀랄 above, the verb was modified with -ㄹ, whereas in 원하는 here, the verb was modified with -는. This is because 놀랄 is in the future tense and 원하는 is in the present tense.

5.

한국에서만큼

= 한국에서 + 만큼

= as much as in Korea

As you can see from the examples above, 만큼 (or -만큼) can be used after various types of words to mean "as much as". However, when 만큼 is used after 얼마, which usually means "how much", 얼마만큼 still has the same meaning of "how much (of something)" or "how much in quantity". In this case, 얼마만큼 can be interchangeable with 얼마나.

Sample Sentences

주연 씨는 경화 씨만큼 키가 커요.

= Jooyeon is as tall as Kyung-hwa.

원하는 만큼 다 가져가세요.

= Take as much as you want.

Track 09

필요한 만큼 가져가세요.

= Take as much as you need.

먹을 만큼만 가져가세요.

= Take just the amount that you will eat.

필요한 만큼만 가져가세요.

= Take just the amount that you need.

한국에서만큼 자주 안 만나요.

= We do not meet as often as in Korea.

얼마만큼 필요해요?

= How much (of it) do you need?

34

How to Say "as much as I would like to..." in Korean

In this case, you cannot use 만큼 to say things like, "As much as I want to go, I cannot." Instead, you need to say 정말 -고 싶지만 which literally means "I really want to, but...".

Ex)

As much as I would like to stay, I must go home.

= 정말 더 있고 싶지만, 집에 가야 돼요.

As much as I would like to go/come, I am too busy.

= 정말 가고 싶지만, 너무 바빠요.

Track 09

35

Sample Dialogue

Track 10

승우: 시험 잘 봤어요?

지원: 공부한 만큼은 못 본 것 같아요.
　　　문제가 너무 어려웠어요.

승우: 그래서 아무것도 못 썼어요?

지원: 그냥 아는 만큼 썼어요.

Seung-woo: Did you do well on your exam?

*Ji-won: I don't think I did as well as I studied.
　　　The questions were too difficult.*

Seung-woo: So you couldn't write anything?

Ji-won: I just wrote as much as I know.

✏ Exercises for Lesson 5

Fill in the blanks with the appropriate Korean word and 만큼 to complete the sentence.

Check the answers on **p.199**

1. (   ) 가져가세요.

    = Take as much as you need.

2. (   ) 가져가세요.

    = Take just the amount that you will eat.

3. (   ) 자주 안 만나요.

    = We do not meet as often as in Korea.

4. 주연 씨는 (   ) 키가 커요.

    = Jooyeon is as tall as Kyung-hwa.

5. (   ) 필요해요?

    = How much (of it) do you need?

LESSON 6

Word Builder 12

원(院)

Track
11

Word Builder lessons are designed to help you understand how to expand your vocabulary by learning and understanding some common and basic building blocks of Korean words. The words and letters introduced through Word Builder lessons are not necessarily all Chinese characters, or 한자. Though many of them are based on Chinese characters, the meanings can be different from modern-day Chinese. Your goal through these lessons is to understand how words are formed and then remember the keywords in Korean to expand your Korean vocabulary from there. You certainly do not have to memorize the Hanja characters, but if you want to, feel free!

Today's key word element is 원.

The Chinese character for this is 院.
There are many other Chinese characters (or Hanja) for 원, so keep in mind that not all the words that have 원 in them have related meanings.

The word 원 (院) is related to "house" and "institute".

38

대 (big) + 학 (study) + 원 (house) = 대학원 大學院 = graduate school

병 (sickness, illness) + 원 (house) = 병원 病院 = hospital

원 (house) + 장 (head) = 원장 院長 = head of an organization or an institute whose name ends with -원

Related Vocabulary
병원장 病院長 = head of a hospital
교장 校長 = principal of a school

학 (study) + 원 (house) = 학원 學院 = private school, institute
* Most Korean students go to a private cram school every day after school where they study with a private teacher. When they are young, they might go to some 학원s to learn subjects that are not taught in schools, such as ballet, taekwondo, or piano; as they grow older, they focus on getting good scores at school, so they prepare and review school subjects such as math and English. Often, 학원 is one of the first words people from other countries learn how to say in Korean.

Track 11

연수 (training, education) + 원 (house) = 연수원 研修院 = training institute

퇴 (to retreat, to go back) + 원 (house) = 퇴원 退院 = leaving the hospital, being discharged from the hospital

Related Vocabulary
퇴실 退室 = to check out of a room, to leave a room for the day
퇴장 退場 = to leave the stage after performing

입 (to enter) + 원 (house) = 입원 入院 = being hospitalized, hospitalization

Related Vocabulary
입장 入場 = to enter the stage

법 (law) + 원 (house) = 법원 法院 = court of law

연구 (research) + 원 (house) = 연구원 研究院 = research center

Related Vocabulary
연구실 研究室 = research room

고 (lonely) + 아 (child) + 원 (house) = 고아원 孤兒院 = orphanage

**Track
11**

Sample Dialogue

Track 12

영주: 무슨 일 하세요?

현우: 학원을 운영하고 있어요.

영주: 아! 학원 원장님이시군요.

현우: 네. 맞아요.

Yeongjoo: What do you do?

Hyunwoo: I am running a private school.

Yeongjoo: Oh! You are the head of a private school!

Hyunwoo: Yes. That's right.

41

✎ Exercises for Lesson 6

Fill in the blanks with the appropriate Sino-Korean word from the lesson.

1. The key word element (   ) is related to "house" and "institute".

2. (   ) = graduate school

3. (   ) = hospital

4. (   ) = being hospitalized, hospitalization

5. (   ) = court of law

Check the answers on **p.199**

Tell Stories, Express Ideas, and

LESSON 7

Even if…, There is no use…

-아/어/여 봤자

Track 13

In today's lesson, we will look at the structure **-아/어/여 봤자** which is used to express the meaning "even if" or "there is no use". It is more commonly used in spoken Korean than in written Korean.

Other similar expressions are -아/어/여도 and -아/어/여 봐도, but these expressions tend to be a little more formal and less intense in nuance than -아/어/여 봤자.

When used after verb stems, -아/어/여 봤자 gives the entire sentence the meaning that "even if" one tries to do something, they will NOT get the desired result.

Take a look at some examples:

말하다 = to talk, to speak
→ 말해 봤자 = Even if you talk (to them) (there is no use).

43

찾다 = to look for, to find

→ 찾아 봤자 = Even if you look for something / even if you find it (there is no use).

How to Say, "It is no use" or, "It will not work."

After you say -아/어/여 봤자, it is already expected that you are going to say something along the lines of, "It will not work", "It is impossible", or, "You cannot do it", but in order to make it clearer, you can use the following expressions:

I. 소용없어요.

= It is of no use. It will not help.

Track 13

2. 안 돼요.

= It will not work. It will not do. You cannot do it.

3. 시간 낭비예요.

= It is a waste of time.

Or you can simply add negative phrases using 안 or 못.

Ex)
말해 봤자 소용없어요.

= Even if you talk (to them), it will be of no use.

가 봤자 시간 낭비예요.

= Even if you go, it will be a waste of your time.

Quite often, you can just drop the above expressions after using -아/어/여 봤자 and just add -예요 (= to be) to end the sentence (-아/어/여 봤자예요). This is because adding -예요 will make it a complete sentence, even though the meaning is clear with just -아/어/여 봤자.

Ex)

해 봤자예요. = There is no use in trying to do it.

가 봤자예요. = There is no use in going there.

Sample Sentences

저한테 말해 봤자 소용없어요.

= There is no use in talking to me.

= 저한테 말해 봤자예요.

Track 13

여기에 있어 봤자 시간 낭비예요.

= Even if you stay here, it is a waste of time.

= 여기에 있어 봤자예요.

지금 출발해 봤자 시간 안에 못 가요.

= Even if you leave now, you cannot get there in time.

= 지금 출발해 봤자예요.

울어 봤자 소용없어요.

= Even if you cry, it will not help.

= 울어 봤자예요.

모르는 척해 봤자 이미 다 알고 있어요.

= Even if you pretend you do not know, I already know all about it.

= 모르는 척해 봤자예요.

45

-아/어/여 봤자 can be replaced with -아/어/여 봐야 when it is followed by a phrase that is NOT -예요 (you cannot say -아/어/여 봐야예요).

Ex)

저한테 말해 봐야 소용없어요.

여기에 있어 봐야 시간 낭비예요.

지금 출발해 봐야 시간 안에 못 가요.

울어 봐야 소용없어요.

모르는 척 해 봐야 이미 다 알고 있어요.

Track 13

46

Sample Dialogue

Track 14

미래: 어? 오빠, 안녕하세요. 주말인데 왜 학교 왔어요?

경석: 집에 있어 봤자 할 일도 없어서 왔어.

미래: 언제까지 있을 거예요?

경석: 저녁까지 있으려고. 일찍 가 봤자 아무도 없어.

Mirae: Huh? Hi Kyung-seok! Why did you come to school on the weekend?

Kyung-seok: There's nothing to do even if I am home, so I came here.

Mirae: Until when will you be here?

Kyung-seok: I am going to stay here until the evening. There is no one at home even if I go there early.

47

✏️ Exercises for Lesson 7

Fill in the blanks with the appropriate Korean word using -**아/어/여 봤자** *to complete the sentence.*

1. ( ) 소용없어요.

= Even if you cry, it will not help.

2. ( ) 이미 다 알고 있어요.

= Even if you pretend you do not know, I already know all about it.

3. 여기에 ( ) 시간 낭비예요.

= Even if you stay here, it is a waste of time.

4. 저한테 ( ) 소용없어요.

= There is no use in talking to me.

5. 지금 ( ) 시간 안에 못 가요.

= Even if you leave now, you cannot get there in time.

Check the answers on **P.200**

LESSON 8

I saw that..., so...

-길래

In this lesson, let us look at the structure **-길래**. -길래 basically expresses a reason why an action is done, but mostly in situations when you have intentionally done something as a result of observing and judging.

You can use -길래 mainly when you are talking about (1) doing something as a result of observation, (2) doing something as a result of judging a situation, or (3) asking the reason/background for a decision. Since you usually talk about the reason for an action and the reason together, the sentence is usually in the past or present tense. With -길래 you usually cannot use it with future tense.

> *Structure*
>
> Verb stem + **-길래** + Result action

Usages

1. Doing something as a result of observation

49

Ex)

비가 오다 (= to rain)

→ 비가 오길래

→ 비가 오길래 우산을 가져왔어요.

(= It was raining so I brought my umbrella.)

　　* You can also say, "비가 와서 우산을 가져왔어요" or, "비가 오니까 우산을 가져왔어요", but if you say, "비가 오길래 우산을 가져왔어요", you can show your intention or observation better.

맛있다 (= to be delicious)

→ 맛있길래

→ 맛있길래 더 사왔어요.

(= It was delicious so I bought some more.)

Track 15

사람이 많다 (= to be crowded)

→ 사람이 많길래

→ 사람이 많길래 그냥 나왔어요.

(= There were a lot of people so I just left the place.)

2. Doing something as a result of judging a situation

Ex)

비가 올 것 같다 (= to seem like it is going to rain)

→ 비가 올 것 같길래

→ 비가 올 것 같길래 그냥 집에 있었어요.

(= It looked like it was going to rain, so I just stayed home.)

Tell Stories, Express Ideas, and

곧 문을 닫을 것 같다 (= to seem like they will close the door soon)

→ 곧 문을 닫을 것 같길래

→ 서점이 곧 문을 닫을 것 같길래 그냥 돌아왔어요.

(= The bookstore looked like it was going to close soon so I just came back.)

* In these situations, you are using your judgment and could actually be wrong.

3. Asking the reason/background for a decision

Ex)

어디에 있다 (= to be where)

→ 어디에 있길래

→ 지금 어디에 있길래 이렇게 시끄러워요?

(= Where are you now? It is so noisy (as a result of that)!)

Track 15

* If you just say, "이렇게 시끄러워요 (= It is so noisy)", it is not a question, so you cannot put a question mark after it. However, since we added 어디에, the whole sentence becomes a question.

뭐 했다 (= to have done what)

→ 뭐 했길래

→ 뭐 했길래 이렇게 지쳤어요?

(= What did you do to be so tired?)

* Sometimes, if the following action or state after -길래 is understood, you do not have to finish it. You can simply say, "뭐 했길래."

뭐라고 말했다 (= to have said what)

→ 뭐라고 말했길래

→ 경화 씨가 뭐라고 말했길래 이렇게 신났어요?

(= What did Kyung-hwa say to make you so excited?)

주연 씨가 뭐라고 말했길래 이렇게 화났어요?

= What did Jooyeon say to make you so angry?

Sample Sentences

무슨 이야기를 들었길래 그렇게 열심히 공부해요?

= What kind of story did you hear to (make you) study so hard?

= What did they tell you? Why are you studying so hard?

어디에 가길래 그렇게 짐을 많이 싸요?

= Where are you going to be packing so much?

= Where are you going? You are packing so much stuff!

누구를 만나길래 그렇게 화장을 열심히 해요?

= Who are you meeting to be putting on so much make-up?

= Why are you putting in so much effort on your make-up? Who are you meeting?

너무 피곤하길래 그냥 집에 있었어요.

= I was too tired, so I just stayed home.

= I realized I was too tired, so I just stayed home.

주연 씨가 아이언맨을 좋아하길래, 아이언맨 피규어를 사 줬어요.

= I saw that Jooyeon likes Iron Man, so I bought her an Iron Man figure.

Sample Dialogue

Track 16

경은: 여러분, 떡볶이 드세요.

경화: 우와! 맛있겠다.

경은: 망원시장에서 이 떡볶이를 먹어
봤는데 너무 맛있길래 사 왔어요.

석진: 그렇지 않아도 이 집 떡볶이가 엄청
유명하길래 먹어 보고 싶었는데! 잘
먹겠습니다.

Kyeong-eun: Everyone, have some tteokbokki.

Kyung-hwa: Wow! It looks yummy!

*Kyeong-eun: I tried this tteokbokki at Mangwon
market and it was really good, so I bought it.*

*Seokjin: Actually I also wanted to try this tteokbokki
because it is really famous! Thank you for
the treat.*

✏ Exercises for Lesson 8

Fill in the blanks with the appropriate Korean word using -길래 to complete the sentence.

Check the answers on **p.200**

1. 뭐 (   ) 이렇게 지쳤어요?

    = What did you do to be so tired?

2. 어디에 (   ) 그렇게 짐을 많이 싸요?

    = Where are you going to be packing so much?

3. 비가 (   ) 그냥 집에 있었어요.

    = It looked like it was going to rain, so I just stayed home.

4. 지금 어디에 (   ) 이렇게 시끄러워요?

    = Where are you now? It is so noisy (as a result of that)!

5. 사람이 (   ) 그냥 나왔어요.

    = There were a lot of people so I just left the place.

LESSON 9

Because one was -ing

-느라고

Track
17

In this lesson, we will take a look at the verb ending -느라고, which is used to link two verbs or actions as a reason for a result. There are other expressions in Korean that you can use, but -느라고 is specifically for when the result is somewhat negative and you want to mention an excuse or reason.

> ### Structure:
> Action + -느라고 + Action/State

The verb that comes before -느라고 should be an action.
(ex. 먹다, 잡다, 읽다, 일하다, etc.)

The verb that comes after -느라고, however, can be either an action or a state.

Ex)
일하다 + -느라고 + 못 가다
(work) + -느라고 + (cannot go)

55

일하느라고 못 갔어요.

= I could not go because I was working.

= I was working so I could not go.

* Here, 일하다 is your excuse/reason for not being able to go somewhere.

-느라고 is usually associated with negative or undesirable results, but you can sometimes use it in a more neutral sense to mention a goal or an objective.

Ex)

시험 준비(를) 하느라고 바빠요.

= I am busy preparing for an exam.

먹을 것을 찾느라고 잠깐 냉장고를 열었어요.

= I opened the refrigerator for a little bit to look for something to eat.

Track
17

The tense of the entire sentence is expressed through the second verb, so you can only use -느라고 with the verb stem of the first verb.

Ex)

준비(를) 했느라고 (x)

준비(를) 하느라고 (o)

가겠느라고 (x)

가느라고 (o)

Sample Sentences

운동하느라고 전화 온 줄 몰랐어요.

= I was working out so I did not know that you had called.

= I was working out so I did not know I received a phone call.

청소하느라고 계속 집에 있었어요.

= I was cleaning so I stayed home all day.

= I stayed home all day because I was cleaning.

뭐 하느라고 이렇게 늦었어요?

= What were you doing to be so late?

= Why are you so late?

* "뭐 하느라고" is a fixed expression.

뭐 하느라고 전화를 안 받아요?

= What were you doing to not answer my calls?

Track 17

그때 아마 일하느라고 바쁠 거예요. 그래도 연락해 보세요.

= At that time, I will probably be busy working. But still try calling me.

학비를 내느라고 돈을 다 썼어요.

= I spent all the money paying my tuition fees.

Instead of the full -느라고, you can also use -느라.

Ex)
운동하느라 전화 온 줄 몰랐어요.
청소하느라 계속 집에 있었어요.
뭐 하느라 이렇게 늦었어요?
뭐 하느라 전화를 안 받아요?

57

그때 아마 일하느라 바쁠 거예요. 그래도 연락해 보세요.

학비를 내느라 돈을 다 썼어요.

Two More Things to Remember:

1. The subject of the two verbs should be the same when you use -느라고.

    Ex)

    친구가 일하느라, 저는 여기 있었어요. (x)

    친구가 일해서, 저는 여기 있었어요. (o)

2. You cannot make an imperative or a "let us" sentence using -느라고.

Track 17

    Ex)

    지금 쇼핑 하느라, 같이 가자. (x)

    지금 쇼핑 할 거니까, 같이 가자. (o)

Sample Dialogue

Track 18

석진: 여보세요.

주연: 계속 전화했는데, 뭐 하느라고 전화 못 받았어요?

석진: 죄송해요. 청소하느라고 진동 소리를 못 들었어요. 무슨 일이에요?

Seokjin: Hello.

Jooyeon: I kept calling you. What were you doing to not answer my calls?

Seokjin: I am sorry. I was vacuuming so I couldn't hear the phone vibrating. What's up?

✏️ *Exercises for Lesson* **9**

Fill in the blanks with the appropriate Korean word using -느라고 *to complete the sentence.*

1. 뭐 (   ) 이렇게 늦었어요?

   = What were you doing to be so late?

2. (   ) 못 갔어요.

   = I could not go because I was working.

3. 학비를 (   ) 돈을 다 썼어요.

   = I spent all the money paying my tuition fees.

4. (   ) 전화 온 줄 몰랐어요.

   = I was working out so I did not know that you had called.

Check the answers on **p.200**

LESSON **10**

Sentence Building Drill 9

Sentence Building Drill 9

In this series, we focus on how you can use the grammatical rules and expressions that you have learned so far to train yourself to comfortably and flexibly make more Korean sentences.

Track
19

We will start off with THREE key sentences, then practice changing parts of these sentences so that you do not end up just memorizing the same three sentences. We want you to be able to be as flexible as possible with the Korean sentences that you can make.

Key Sentence (1)

그 사람은 지금 음악 듣느라고, 아무리 불러 봤자 못 들어요.

= He is listening to music now so no matter how much you try to call him, he cannot hear you.

Key Sentence (2)

뭐라고 말했길래 그 사람이 저를 모르는 척해요?

= What did you say to make him pretend not to know me?

61

Key Sentence (3)

제가 말한 것처럼 했군요!

= You really did like I said!

Expansion & Variation Practice with Key Sentence (I)

0. Original Sentence:

그 사람은 지금 음악 듣느라고, 아무리 불러 봤자 못 들어요.

= He is listening to music now so no matter how much you try to call him, he cannot hear you.

Track 19

I.

그 사람은 지금 음악 듣느라고 = He is listening to music now so...

저 지금 전화 받느라고 = I am talking on the phone now so...

아까 텔레비전 보느라고 = I was watching TV earlier so...

시험 공부 하느라고 = I was studying for an exam so...

2.

아무리 불러 봤자 못 들어요. = No matter how hard you try to call him, he cannot hear you.

아무리 노력해 봤자 안 돼요. = No matter how much effort you make, you cannot do it.

아무리 걱정해 봤자 소용없어요. = No matter how much you worry, it is of no use.

아무리 서둘러 봤자 이미 늦었어요.* = No matter how much we hurry up, we are already late.

* In English, you use the word "late" in the present tense, but in Korean, you say it in the past tense although you are talking about the present.

Expansion & Variation Practice with Key Sentence (2)

0. Original Sentence:

뭐라고 말했길래 그 사람이 저를 모르는 척해요?

= What did you say to make him pretend not to know me?

1.

뭐라고 말했길래 = What did you say to...

아침에 비가 오길래 = I saw that it was raining in the morning so...

집에 우유가 없길래 = I found that there was no milk at home so...

조용하길래 = I realized that it was quiet so...

2.

그 사람이 저를 모르는 척해요. = He pretends not to know me.

저랑 친한 척하지 마세요. = Do not pretend you are close friends with me.

그냥 바쁜 척했어요. = I just pretended I was busy.

걱정 없는 척했어요. = I pretended I was not worried.

Track
19

Expansion & Variation Practice with Key Sentence (3)

0. Original Sentence:

제가 말한 것처럼 했군요!

= You really did like I said!

1.

제가 말한 것처럼 = like (what) I said

우리 어제 이야기한 것처럼 = like we discussed yesterday

영화 배우처럼 = like a movie actor

처음처럼 = like the beginning

2.

했군요 = I see that you did it!

그랬군요 = I see THAT is what happened.

한국에 오래 살았군요 = I see that you have lived in Korea for a long time.

이게 제일 좋은 거군요 = I see that this is the best one.

**Track
19**

Sample Dialogue

Track 20

경화: 우와! 현우 씨 그림 잘 그리시네요.

현우: 아니에요. 제가 아무리 잘 그려 봤자 경화 씨처럼은 못 그리죠.

경화: 네? 제 그림을 언제 보셨길래 제가 그림을 잘 그린다고 생각하세요?

현우: 이 그림 경화 씨가 그린 거 아니에요?

Kyung-hwa: Wow! You are good at drawing!

Hyunwoo: Not really. No matter how good I am at drawing, I can't draw as well as you.

Kyung-hwa: Sorry? When did you see my drawing that made you think I am good at drawing?

Hyunwoo: Isn't this drawing done by you?

✏ Exercises for Lesson 10

Translate each phrase or sentence into Korean and write it on the lines provided.

1. like (what) I said

....

2. I just pretended I was busy.

....

3. I found that there was no milk at home so...

....

4. No matter how much you worry, it is of no use.

....

5. No matter how much we hurry up, we are already late.

....

Check the answers on **p.200**

BLOG

Pajeon (파전) Recipe

I love Korean food, especially the ones that I can make at home and tailor to my tastes. One such food is pajeon (파전) or "Korean pancake". The word "pa" means scallion in Korean, while "jeon" refers to a dish that typically includes some sort of chopped or minced meat mixed with wheat flour and egg wash before being fried. This is typically a side dish or a great meal to have with some makgeolli. One of the best things about this dish is there are so many different ways you can prepare it. If you do not eat meat, there is kimchijeon or gamjajeon. Gamja (감자) means potato. If you do eat meat, you can try seafood pajeon (해물파전), which includes different kinds of seafood. However, you can add or take away just about anything to tailor it to your style. So, today what I would like to do is give you the recipe to make your own pajeon. Do not worry, this is super easy to make and as long as you follow the steps, you will be enjoying your very own pajeon at home, bringing a bit of Korea to your doorstep. This recipe is also a great way to impress your friends if you are having a dinner at your place.

One thing about Korean recipes is that people tend to simply use their eyes when measuring what is needed. They say to taste it and if it is not right, then add more of what you think is missing. However, to make things easier for you, we have a recipe for you to use. Now, with pajeon, you can take out some of the things you do not like and even add things you might want. For instance, my wife and I like perilla leaves (깻잎), so a lot of the time, we will add it to some of the dishes we like; pajeon is one of those dishes. If you do not like it though, you can simply leave it out and it will taste just fine. Today's recipe will be seafood pajeon with shrimp and squid. However, you can use other seafood items if you aren't a fan of shrimp or squid!

Ingredients:

14 Stalks of Green Onion

½ Onion

¼ Carrot

⅓ Korean Zucchini

2 Green Peppers

2 Red Chili Peppers

2 Cups Korean Pancake Mix (if you do not have Korean pancake mix, you can use 1 cup cake flour, or you can mix ¾ cup of flour and 2 Tbsp of cornstarch)

2 Cups Tempura Mix

1 Squid

8-12 Shrimp, shells and tails removed

½ cup water

3 Eggs (Optional)

Cooking Oil

Dipping Sauce

¼ Onion

2 Tablespoons Soy Sauce

1 Tablespoon Vinegar

1 Tablespoon Mirim (Cooking Wine)

½ Tablespoon Sugar

1 Tablespoon Water

How to Prepare:

Cut the green onion stalks about an inch in size.

Slice your onions, carrots, and Korean zucchini lengthwise in one inch sizes.

Thinly slice the chili peppers.

Chop the squid into small pieces.

Mix all of the vegetables except the red chili peppers (they will be used later).

Add both the Korean pancake mix (or flour) and tempura mix to your vegetables.

Add the shrimp and squid to the mix.

Now add the water and stir until everything is mixed well.

Preheat a frying pan and add some cooking oil.

Using a ladle, add the mix to your pan and spread it out evenly, making sure everything is covered with the batter.

While your pajeon is cooking, it is time to make the dipping sauce.

Chop up the onion and place into a small bowl.

Add the soy sauce, vinegar, mirim, sugar, and water.

Stir.

Now that we have our sauce, flip the pajeon over to cook the other side. Once both sides are cooked (making sure the squid and shrimp have been fully cooked), you are now ready to eat your own seafood pajeon!

If you would like to see a video with step-by-step instructions, you can check out Yoon Johnny's video where he made buchujeon, which is quite similar to seafood pajeon. Some of the ingredients will be different, but the technique is very similar.

🔗 https://youtu.be/Zakyw4fjk_U

Written by Johnny Bland

LESSON 11

Making Things Happen (Causative Verbs)

-이/히/리/기/우/구/추-

Track 21

In English, when you want to say "make someone do something" or "make something do something", you need to add that extra word "make", or other words such as "let", "have", etc. However, in Korean, this works in a slightly different way. In Level 6 Lesson 21, we introduced the suffixes -이/히/리/기- that make a verb "passive voice". These same suffixes are also used to convert a regular verb into a causative verb.

Causative suffixes:

-이-

-히-

-리-

-기-

-우-

-구-

-추-

There are general rules for which suffix to use, but there are also a lot of exceptions, so it is best to learn by trial and error as well as by looking at a lot of common examples.

Not all verbs, however, can be changed into causative verbs by adding these suffixes. You cannot form a causative verb with -이/히/리/기/우/구/추- when the verb is already a transitive verb. For example, "to push" is 밀다 in Korean and is already a transitive verb. So if you add -리 to it and make it 밀리다, it changes into the passive voice, "to be pushed".

At first, it will be easier for you to "understand" these suffixes than to "use" them. When a certain verb does not work with these suffixes, you can still change it into the causative form by adding -게 하다. An example of such a verb is 가다. 가다 cannot work with -이/히/리/기/우/구/추-, so you can only conjugate it as 가게 하다 to say "to make someone go".

Track 21

All verbs can be changed into the causative form by using -게 하다.
Some verbs can be changed into the causative form by using -이/히/리/기/우/구/추-; these verbs are more commonly used with -이/히/리/기/우/구/추- than with -게 하다.

1. -이-
-이- is used mostly after a vowel or sometimes after ㄱ.

Ex)
녹다 = to melt / 녹이다 = to make something melt, to melt something
보다 = to see / 보이다 = to show
높다 = to be high / 높이다 = to make something higher, to heighten

2. -히-
-히- is used mostly after ㄱ, ㄷ, or ㅂ.

Ex)

입다 = to wear / 입히다 = to make someone wear something

읽다 = to read / 읽히다 = to make someone read something

앉다 = to sit / 앉히다 = to seat someone, to make someone sit

밝다 = to be bright / 밝히다 = to brighten

3. -리-

-리- is used mostly after ㄹ or ㄷ irregular.

Ex)

울다 = to cry / 울리다 = to make someone cry

놀다 = to play / 놀리다 = to let/make someone play, to tease

Track 21

4. -기-

-기- is used mostly after ㄴ, ㅁ, or ㅅ.

Ex)

신다 = to wear (shoes) / 신기다 = to make someone wear (shoes/socks)

안다 = to hug / 안기다 = to make someone hug someone

5. -우/구/추-

-우/구/추- have too many exceptions to generalize the rule.

낮다 = to be low / 낮추다 = to lower, to make something lower

맞다 = to fit / 맞추다 = to make something fit, to have something tailor-made

자다 = to sleep / 재우다 = to make someone sleep

크다 = to be big / 키우다 = to make something bigger, to grow

차다 = to be filled up / 채우다 = to fill

하다 and 시키다

If you remember from the passive voice lessons, 하다 changes to 되다 when you make it passive. When you want to use 하다 and say "make someone do something", you can use the word 시키다. This can also be applied to many "Noun + -하다" verbs.

Ex)
공부하다 = to study / 공부시키다 = to make someone study
준비하다 = to prepare / 준비시키다 = to get someone ready

Sample Sentences

아이들 울리지 마세요.

= Do not make the kids cry.

너무 높으니까 좀 낮춰 주세요.

= It is too high, so lower it a little.

   * You cannot say, "낮아 주세요." You cannot use imperative conjugations with an adjective.

다른 것도 보여 주세요.

= Show me some other things, too.

   * If you say, "다른 것도 봐 주세요", it means, "Please look at some other things."

제가 너무 바빠서 다른 사람한테 시켰어요.

= I was too busy so I made another person do it.

아이 세 명을 키우고 있어요.

= I am raising three kids.

75

Even More Examples

1. 좁다 = to be narrow / 좁히다 = to make something narrower

2. 넓다 = to be wide / 넓히다 = to widen

3. 남다 = to remain / 남기다 = to leave (a comment), to leave something over

4. 숨다 = to hide / 숨기다 = to hide something, to make something hidden

5. 넘다 = to go over / 넘기다 = to make something go over something

Track 21

Tell Stories, Express Ideas, and

Sample Dialogue

솔미: 하은이는 진짜 순한 아이 같아요.
하은이처럼 순하면 열 명도 키우겠어요.

소희: 하은이요? 평소에는 순한데 재울 때
너무 힘들어요.

솔미: 왜요?

소희: 침대에 눕히려고 하면 울어요. 그래서
매일 업고 재워서 허리가 너무 아파요.

Solmi: Ha-eun seems like such a sweet kid. If my kids were sweet like Ha-eun, I could even raise ten of them.

Sohee: Ha-eun? She is usually sweet, but it is really hard when I put her to sleep.

Solmi: Why?

Sohee: If I am about to lay her on the bed, she cries. So, I put her to sleep by piggy-back every day, so my back hurts a lot.

Check the answers on **p.200**

✏ Exercises for Lesson 11

Convert each verb into a causative verb.

1. 좁다 →

2. 낮다 →

3. 울다 →

4. 신다 →

5. 넘다 →

6. 자다 →

7. 밝다 →

8. 높다 →

9. 넓다 →

10. 크다 →

LESSON **12**

Retelling/Reporting on Speech

-더라(고요)

In this lesson, we will take a look at the verb ending **-더라**. You will hear this often in situations where one person is telling another what they found out or experienced.

What is -더라?

-더라 is used when you tell someone else about a new fact that you learned by experiencing (i.e. seeing, finding, realizing, etc.) it yourself.

Let us take a look at some examples:

예쁘다 = to be pretty
예뻐요 = (She/It is) pretty.
→ 예쁘 + -더라 = 예쁘더라 = She is pretty! / I saw her, and she is so pretty!

춥다 = to be cold
추워요 = It is cold.

→ 춥 + -더라 = 춥더라 = It was so cold! / I went there, and it was so cold!
* You could say, "추워요", but, "춥더라" has more emphasis.

Like in the examples above, when you use -더라, it should be about a past action because you are talking about something that you have already experienced.

What is the difference between -더라, -더라고 and -더라고요?

They all mean -더라, but by adding -고 you slightly change the meaning. When you use -더라, you are telling someone a fact about something based on what you saw or experienced, but in a more 'exclamatory' way. When you use -더라고 instead of -더라, the tone of your sentence is calmer, and it sounds less excited and conclusive than when you say -더라. If you add -요 to -더라고, it makes the sentence more polite.

Track 23

> **Ex)**
> 나는 그거 좋더라. = (I checked it out and) I liked it! [Very excited]
> 나는 그거 좋더라고. = (I checked it out and) I liked it. [More calm and neutral]

How do you say -더라 in 존댓말?

You can change -더라고 to 존댓말 quite easily just by adding -요 at the end. With -더라, however, it is a little bit different. You need to use the ending -던데요.

예쁘더라. → 예쁘던데요.
빠르더라. → 빠르던데요.

Naturally, you can also change it back to 반말 by getting rid of -요 at the end of -던데요.

Tell Stories, Express Ideas, and

Sample Sentences

그 영화 어제 봤는데, 재미있더라! (재미있던데요!/재미있더라고!/재미있더라고요!)

= I saw that movie yesterday, and it was fun!

어제 경화 씨 만났는데, 머리를 염색했더라. (염색했던데요./염색했더라고./염색했더라고요.)

= I met Kyung-hwa yesterday, and she had dyed her hair.

* Notice that here we are using "했" since she did it in the past.

싱가포르에 처음 가 봤는데, 정말 덥더라. (덥던데요./덥더라고./덥더라고요.)

= I went to Singapore for the first time, and it was really hot there.

윤아 씨한테 물어봤는데, 모르더라. (모르던데요./모르더라고./모르더라고요.)

= I asked Yoona, and she does not know.

Track
23

아까 주연 씨 만났는데, 친구랑 있더라. (있던데요./있더라고./있더라고요.)

= I met Jooyeon earlier, and she was with her friend.

Remember!

1. -더라 normally does not work with statements about one's own will or action.

Ex)

아침에 일어났는데 내가 바쁘더라. (x)

One case in which you could use this about yourself is for example, if you were an actor and got your script the day you arrived on set.

Ex)

오늘 가 봤는데 내가 형사더라.

= I went today, and found out I was a detective.

Typically, you wouldn't use this ending when talking about yourself.

2. You can use -더라 about your own emotions, but normally not about other people's emotions.

Ex)

기쁘더라. (o) = I was happy/pleased.

석진 씨가 기쁘더라. (x)

슬프더라. (o) = It was sad (to me). / I was sad.

현우 씨가 슬프더라. (x)

If you use the verb form, though, you can say other people's emotions.

Ex)

석진 씨가 기뻐하더라. = I saw Seokjin, and he was pleased.

현우 씨가 슬퍼하더라. = I saw Hyunwoo, and he was grieving/feeling sad.

3. You can NOT use -더라 if you have NOT experienced, seen, or read about something yourself.

Ex)

콘서트에 갔는데, 가수가 노래를 잘하더라. (o)

콘서트에 못 갔는데, 가수가 노래를 잘하더라. (x)

Sample Dialogue

Track 24

경화: 오늘 오랜만에 홍대 갔는데, 그 카페 없어졌더라.

주연: 무슨 카페?

경화: 네가 자주 가는 카페 있잖아.

주연: 어? 왜 갑자기 없어졌지?

경화: 글쎄. 오늘 보니까 없더라고.

Kyung-hwa: I went to Hongdae today for the first time in a long time, and the café was gone.

Jooyeon: What café?

Kyung-hwa: You know, the café where you often go.

Jooyeon: Huh? Why is it gone all of a sudden?

Kyung-hwa: I don't know. I looked for it today, and it wasn't there.

Check the answers on **p.200**

✏️ *Exercises for Lesson 12*

Rewrite the sentences that end in -**았/었/였어** *using* -**더라** *so they sound more exclamatory.*

1. 그 영화 어제 봤는데, 재미있었어.

→

2. 어제 경화 씨 만났는데, 머리를 염색했어.

→

3. 싱가포르에 처음 가 봤는데, 정말 더웠어.

→

4. 윤아 씨한테 물어봤는데, 몰랐어.

→

5. 아까 주연 씨 만났는데, 친구랑 있었어.

→

Tell Stories, Express Ideas, and

LESSON **13**

Word Builder 13

기(機)

Word Builder lessons are designed to help you understand how to expand your vocabulary by learning and understanding some common and basic building blocks of Korean words. The words and letters introduced through Word Builder lessons are not necessarily all Chinese characters, or 한자. Though many of them are based on Chinese characters, the meanings can be different from modern-day Chinese. Your goal through these lessons is to understand how words are formed and then remember the keywords in Korean to expand your Korean vocabulary from there. You certainly do not have to memorize the Hanja characters, but if you want to, feel free!

Track 25

Today's key word element is 기.

The Chinese character for this is 機.
There are many other Chinese characters (or Hanja) for 기, so keep in mind that not all the words that have 기 in them have related meanings.

The word 기 (機) is related to "frame", "machine", or "loom".

85

기 (frame) + 계 (machine) = 기계 機械 = machine

* Remember, you cannot use 기 (機) by itself to say "machine." You have to say 기계 (機械).

기 (frame) + 회 (to meet) = 기회 機會 = opportunity, chance

비 (to fly) + 행 (to go about) + 기 (machine) = 비행기 飛行機 = airplane

기 (airplane) + 내 (inside) + 식 (food, meal) = 기내식 機內食 = in-flight meal

* 기 (機) here refers to the previous word, 비행기 (飛行機), or airplane.

세 (to wash) + 탁 (to wash) + 기 (machine) = 세탁기 洗濯機 = washing machine

* 세 and 탁 used together means "the wash".

Track 25

전 (electricity) + 화 (to talk, dialog) + 기 (machine) = 전화기 電話機 = telephone

기 (frame) + 관 (relations) = 기관 機關 = organization

교육 (education) + 기관 (organization) = 교육 기관 敎育 機關 = educational organization

언론 (press) + 기관 (organization) = 언론 기관 言論 機關 = the media, the press

정부 (government) + 기관 (organization) = 정부 기관 政府 機關 = government organization

복 (to overlap) + 사 (to copy) + 기 (machine) = 복사기 複寫機 = copy machine, photocopier

선 (hand fan) + 풍 (wind) + 기 (machine) = 선풍기 扇風機 = electric fan

자 (automatic, self) + 판 (to sell) + 기 (machine) = 자판기 自販機 = vending machine

* This comes from a longer word, "자동판매기 (自動販賣機)".

계 (to count) + 산 (to count) + 기 (machine) = 계산기 計算機 = calculator

발 (to generate, to develop) + 전 (electricity) + 기 (machine) = 발전기 發電機 = electric generator

Track 25

Sample Dialogue

지민: 복사기 새로 샀어요? 좋은데요!

석진: 네. 저희 자판기도 생겼어요.

지민: 우와. 어디에 있어요?

석진: 지민 씨 뒤에 있어요.

Jimin: Did you buy a new copy machine? It looks nice!

Seokjin: Yes. We also have a vending machine now.

Jimin: Wow. Where is it?

Seokjin: It's behind you.

Tell Stories, Express Ideas, and

✎ Exercises for Lesson 13

Fill in the blanks with the appropriate Sino-Korean word from the lesson.

1. The key word element (   ) is related to "frame", "machine", or "loom".

2. (   ) = vending machine

3. (   ) = airplane

4. (   ) = calculator

5. (   ) = copy machine

Check the answers on **p.200**

LESSON 14

No matter how...

아무리 -아/어/여도

Track 27

In this lesson, we will look at how to say "no matter how..." in Korean. To say this, you need to know two key parts: one is the word 아무리, and the other is the suffix -아/어/여도 (introduced in Level 3 Lesson 20).

> ### Conjugation
> 아무리 + Verb Stem + -아/어/여도
> = No matter how + Verb/Adverb/Adjective...

아무리 has a definition, but it is rarely used on its own to define or mean anything. This word is usually used together with -아/어/여도 or other endings that mean "even if" or "however". You COULD say the same thing without 아무리, but 아무리 makes the meaning of the entire sentence much stronger and clearer.

> **Ex)**
> 아무리 바빠도 = No matter how busy you are...
> 아무리 어려워도 = No matter how difficult it is...

90

아무리 심심해도 = No matter how bored you are...

* You can understand the tense and the voice, as well as the subject of the entire sentence, from the context.

Using 아무리 with Nouns

Sometimes you can use 아무리 with nouns, but in order to make them "verbs", you need to add the -이다 verb. For example, if you want to say 부자, "a rich person", you need to change it to 부자이다; -이다 conjugates to either -아/어/여도 or -(이)라도.

Ex)
No matter how rich you are...
= Even if you are a rich person...
= 아무리 부자여도
= 아무리 부자라도

Track 27

More Examples:

아무리 미인이라도
= 아무리 미인이어도
= No matter how much of a beauty she is...

아무리 바보라도
= 아무리 바보여도
= No matter how big of a fool you are...

Using 아무리 With Other Endings

You can express similar meanings with other endings. 아무리 -아/어/여도 can be replaced with 아무리 -어/어/여 봤자 (Level 7 Lesson 7), 아무리 -고 싶어도, 아무리 -려고 해도, 아무리 -(으/느)ㄴ다고 해도, etc. However, the sentences will all have subtle differences based on the core meaning of the second phrase.

Ex)

아무리 공부해도 (most neutral)

= No matter how much you study...

아무리 공부해 봤자 (least hopeful)

= No matter how much you study...

아무리 공부하고 싶어도

= No matter how much you want to study...

아무리 공부하려고 해도

= No matter how much you are going to try to study...

아무리 공부한다고 해도 (less hopeful)

= No matter how much you study...

아무리 + Verb Stem + -아/어/여도 그렇지...

In addition to the basic structure of -아/어/여도, there is another commonly used structure, -아/어/여도 그렇지, that is used with 아무리. When you add "그렇지", the sentence can be used on its own, without a second clause. Here, 그렇지 means "but still...".

Ex)

아무리 어려워도

= No matter how difficult it is...

아무리 어려워도 그렇지.

= I know it is difficult, but still... / No matter how difficult it is, still....

    * If you say 아무리 어려워도, you need to continue your sentence. However, if you say 아무리 어려워도 그렇지, you are leaving off part of the sentence but still getting your point across.

아무리 학생이라도

= Even though he is a student...

아무리 학생이라도 그렇지.

= Even though that person is a student...

Track 27

아무리 바빠도 그렇지. = No matter how busy you are...

By adding -요 at the end, you can make the sentence more polite.

→ 아무리 바빠도 그렇지요.

Note you are using -지요, but when you say it quickly, it becomes -죠.

→ 아무리 바빠도 그렇죠.

Sample Sentences

아무리 늦어도 2시까지는 오세요.

= No matter how late you are, be there by 2.

= Come by 2 at the latest.

아무리 싫어도, 안 싫은 척해 주세요.

= No matter how much you hate him/her, please pretend you do not.

= No matter how much you do not feel like doing this, please pretend you do.

* 싫다 not only means "to hate", but it also means that you do not feel like doing something.

아무리 맛있어도 이제 그만 먹어요.

= No matter how delicious it is, stop eating now.

아무리 비싸도 제가 사 줄게요.

= No matter how expensive it is, I will buy it for you.

Track 27

아무리 학생이라도 공부만 하는 건 아니에요.

= Even if you are a student, you do not always study.

= Even students do not always study.

Sample Dialogue

Track
28

경은: 이 식당은 너무 불친절한 것 같아요.

석진: 맞아요. 너무 심하네요.

경은: 저는 음식이 아무리 맛있어도 불친절한 식당은 다시 오고 싶지 않아요.

석진: 그래요? 저는 아무리 친절해도 음식이 맛없으면 다시 안 가요.

Kyeong-eun: I think people in this restaurant are very rude.

Seokjin: That's right. They are very rude.

Kyeong-eun: I don't want to go to a rude restaurant again no matter how good the food is.

Seokjin: Is that so? I don't go to restaurants again if the food is not good no matter how kind they are.

95

✎ Exercises for Lesson 14

Translate each phrase into Korean using 아무리 -아/어/여도.

1. No matter how delicious it is...

....

2. No matter how much you hate it...

....

3. No matter how busy you are...

....

4. No matter how expensive it is...

....

5. No matter how late you are...

....

Check the answers on **p.201**

LESSON **15**

What was it again?

뭐더라?, 뭐였죠?

Sometimes you forget the name of someone, something, or some place. Sometimes you do not remember what someone else has said or on what date something happened. In those situations, you might ask yourself or say things out loud like, "What was it?", "What was it again?", "What was I going to say?", "Where were we going to meet tonight?", etc. In this lesson, let us take a look at how to say those phrases in Korean.

Key Structures

1. -더라? (Only possible with casual language and speaking to oneself)
2. -았/었/였지? (Only possible with casual language and speaking to oneself)
3. -았/었/였죠? (Only possible with formal language)

Usage of "-더라?" (Only possible with casual language and speaking to oneself)

You can add -더라? at the end of the verb stem of an action verb to say, "I forgot. What was it that...". When you want to use -더라? with a noun, however, you need to change the noun into the verb form by adding -이다.

→ Noun + -이다 (to be) + -더라?

You can drop -이 when the noun ends with a vowel, so therefore for nouns such as 나무, 여자, 남자, 누구, etc., you can simply add -더라? at the end.

Let us take a look at some examples

이거 누구 책이에요? = Whose book is this? / This is whose book?
→ 이거 누구 책이더라? = Whose book was this again? (I forgot,) Whose book is this?

주연 씨 생일이 언제예요? = When is Jooyeon's birthday?
주연 씨 생일이 언제더라? = When was Jooyeon's birthday again? / When is Jooyeon's birthday? (I forgot.)

이거 어떻게 해요? = How do you do this?
이거 어떻게 하더라? = How do you do this? (Can you tell me again?)

Track 29

Usage of "-았/었/였지?" (Only possible with casual language and speaking to oneself)

-았/었/였지? basically has the same usage and construction as -더라?, so you can change the endings of all the example sentences above to -았/었/였지.

이거 누구 책이더라?
→ 이거 누구 책이었지?

주연 씨 생일이 언제더라?

→ 주연 씨 생일이 언제였지?

* Here, this sounds like a past tense sentence, but that is not necessarily the case. Jooyeon's birthday might be coming up in the future, but you can still say this in the past tense. By using the past tense, you are actually referring to the point where you used to remember.

이거 어떻게 하더라?

→ 이거 어떻게 했지?

The meanings are the same, but the latter (using -았/었/였지?) has a slightly stronger nuance toward the past tense.

Usage of "-았/었/였죠?" (Only possible with formal language)

Track 29

-았/었/였죠? is basically the same as -았/었/였지? but is in the 존댓말 form. -았/었/였죠? is originally just -았/었/였지 + 요? but when pronounced quickly and naturally, it becomes -죠 at the end. Therefore, you can use all the example sentences above with -죠? or -지요? at the end to make the sentences more polite and formal.

Usage With -다고 and -라고

Since you can use -더라?, -았/었/였지?, and -았/었/였죠? when checking with someone what something is called or when something is scheduled, etc., you can often hear people say these together with -다고 or -라고. This is because -다고 and -라고 are used in order to 'quote' someone.

Ex)

이거 뭐였죠?

= What was this again? / What is this? (I forgot.)

이거 뭐라고 했죠?

= What did you say this was?

Sample Sentences

석진 씨가 언제 온다고 했죠?

= When did you say Seokjin was going to come? / When did Seokjin say he was going to come?

Track 29

석진 씨가 한국에 언제 왔죠?

= When did Seokjin come to Korea? (I forgot.)

석진 씨가 한국에 언제 오더라?

= When is Seokjin coming to Korea? (I forgot.)

이거 누구 거더라?

= Whose is this? (I forgot.)

이거 누구 거라고 했더라?

= You said this was whose? / Whose did you say this was?

그 사람 이름이 뭐더라?

= What was his name again?

= 그 사람 이름이 뭐였더라?

= 그 사람 이름이 뭐라고 했더라?

Tell Stories, Express Ideas, and

내일 몇 시에 올 거라고 했죠?

= What time did you say you were going to come tomorrow?

이게 한국어로 뭐였죠?

= What was this in Korean again?

Track 29

Hold Deeper Conversations

Sample Dialogue

Track 30

현우: 경화 씨가 싫어하는 아이스크림이 뭐였죠?

석진: 경화 씨는 아이스크림 다 좋아해요.

현우: 아니에요. 어떤 아이스크림 안 좋아한다고 했는데... 뭐더라?

석진: 아! 기억났어요. 바닐라 아이스크림 안 좋아한다고 했어요.

Hyunwoo: What was the ice cream that Kyung-hwa dislikes?

Seokjin: Kyung-hwa likes all ice cream.

Hyunwoo: No. She said she doesn't like some kind of ice cream. What was it?

Seokjin: Ah! I remember! She said she doesn't like vanilla ice cream.

Tell Stories, Express Ideas, and

✏ Exercises for Lesson 15

Rewrite the sentences that end in -**더라**? *using* -**았/었/였지**?, *which means the same thing.*

1. 이거 누구 거더라?

　⟶

2. 그 사람 이름이 뭐더라?

　⟶

3. 주연 씨 생일이 언제더라?

　⟶

4. 이거 누구 책이더라?

　⟶

5. 이게 한국어로 뭐더라?

　⟶

Check the answers on **p.201**

LESSON 16

I said...

-다니까(요), -라니까(요)

Track 31

In this lesson, let us take a look at how to say things like, "I said so!", "I told you!", "I told you that this is...", or, "I said that I am..." in Korean, repeating and emphasizing what you have already said before. In Korean, the key ending used to express this is **-다니까(요)/라니까(요)**. You can use this ending not only to repeat what you have said before, but also to make your point clearer by emphasizing it one more time. For a review of how to say "I said that I..." in a more neutral tone, check out Level 6, Lesson 11.

Using -다니까(요) with Verbs

In the present tense, descriptive verbs and action verbs are followed by different endings.

After descriptive verbs, you just add -다니까(요).

Ex)
바쁘다 = to be busy
바쁘 + 다니까요 = I told you I am busy. / I said I am busy.

104

— 바쁘다니까요! (polite/formal)

— 바쁘다니까! (casual)

After action verbs, you add -(느)ㄴ다니까(요). You add -는다니까(요) after a verb stem ending with a consonant and -ㄴ다니까(요) after a verb stem ending with a vowel.

Ex)

모르다 = to not know

모르 + -ㄴ다니까요 = I told you I do not know. / I said I do not know.

— 모른다니까요! (polite/formal)

— 모른다니까! (casual)

먹다 = to eat

먹 + -는다니까요 = I told you I am going to eat. / I said I am eating.

Track 31

— 먹는다니까요! (polite/formal)

— 먹는다니까! (casual)

In the past tense, both descriptive verbs and action verbs are followed by the same suffixes, -았/었/였 and then -다니까(요).

Ex)

몰랐다니까요. = I said I did not know.

벌써 다 했다니까요. = I told you I already did it all.

진짜 맛있었다니까요. = I told you it was really delicious.

Using -(이)라니까(요) with Nouns

After nouns, you need to add -(이)라니까(요). You add -이라니까(요) after nouns ending with a consonant and -라니까(요) after nouns ending with a vowel. Since the future tense is expressed through "Verb stem + -을 거" and the word 거 is a noun, the future tense is also followed by -라니까(요).

> **Ex)**
> 학생 = student
> 학생 + -이라니까요 = I said I am a student.
>
> 가다 = to go
> 갈 거예요 = I will go.
> 갈 거라니까요 = I told you I am going to go.
> * 갈 거 is a noun group. So, if you think of it as a noun, you just add -라니까요.

Using -(으)라니까(요) with Imperative

With imperatives*, you need to add -(으)라니까(요) after the verb stem. You add -으라니까(요) after verb stems ending with a consonant and -라니까(요) after verb stems ending with a vowel.

* When you tell someone to do something

> **Ex)**
> 보다 = to look
> 보 + -라니까(요) = I said look!
> * If you want to say, "I said I am looking", you have to say, "본다니까요."

Track 31

106

잡다 = to grab

잡 + -(으)라니까(요) = I said grab it!

Sample Sentences

빨리 오라니까요.

= I said come here quickly!

빨리 온다니까요.

= I said I am coming quickly.

빨리 왔다니까요.

= I said they came here quickly.

Track 31

알았다니까요!

= I said I got it!

= I said I understood!

제가 안 했다니까요.

= I said I did not do it!

저 안 한다니까요.

= I am not doing it.

저는 죄가 없다니까요.

= I told you I am innocent.

혼자 갈 거라니까요.

= I said I am going alone!

혼자 갔다니까요.

= I said I went there alone.

저는 정말 몰랐다니까요.

= I said I really did not know.

매일 운동한다니까요.

= I said I exercise every day.

Track 31

다음 달부터 열심히 공부할 거라니까요.

= I said I am going to study hard starting next month!

그럴 수도 있다니까요.

= I said it is possible too.

공부 좀 하라니까요.

= I said, "Do some studying!"

Tell Stories, Express Ideas, and

Sample Dialogue

동생: 추석 기차표 예매했어?

언니: 이번 추석에 일 있어서 못 내려간다니까.

동생: 나 혼자 갈 거라니까.

언니: 그럼 네가 예매해.

Younger sister: Have you booked the train tickets for Chuseok?

Older sister: I said I can't go this Chuseok because I've got something to do.

Younger sister: I told you I would go by myself.

Older sister: Then, YOU book your ticket.

Check the answers on **p.201**

🖊 Exercises for Lesson 16

Rewrite the sentences using -**다니까요** *or* -**라니까요** *as if you are repeating and emphasizing what you have already said.*

1. 몰라요.

→

2. 바빠요.

→

3. 혼자 갈 거예요.

→

4. 제가 안 했어요.

→

4. 저는 정말 몰랐어요.

→

110

LESSON 17

I heard..., They say that...

-(ㄴ/는)대요, -(이)래요

Let us take a look at how to say "They say...", "I hear that...", or how to re-tell someone what you have heard from someone else. There are mainly two ways of saying this in Korean, through the endings **-(ㄴ/는)대요** and **-(이)래요.** These endings might sound complicated, but in fact, they are just combinations of grammar points that you have already learned before.

In Level 5 Lesson 17, you learned the following grammar points:

-(ㄴ/는)다고
-(이)라고

These are used for quoting what someone has said and are also used with verbs related to speech. In that lesson, we introduced the following sample sentences:

뭐라고 했어요? = What did they say?
내일 온다고 했어요. = (Someone) said they would come tomorrow.

Track 33

언제 온다고 했어요? = When did they say they would come?

이거 재미있다고 들었어요. = I heard that this is fun.

You can make all of the above sentences shorter by using the endings -(ㄴ/는)대(요) and -(이)래(요).

-(ㄴ/는)다고 해요 → -(ㄴ/는)대요

-(이)라고 해요 → -(이)래요

Although it is basically the same thing, the latter forms are more commonly used in everyday spoken Korean because they are shorter and much easier to pronounce.

Conjugation

Track 33

Present Tense:

Action Verbs + -(느)ㄴ대요

Ex) 지금 간대요. (= They say they are going now.)

Descriptive Verbs + -대요

Ex) 바쁘대요. (= He says that he is busy now.)

Nouns + -(이)래요

Ex) 친구래요. (= She says that he is a friend.)

Past Tense:

Action Verbs + -았/었/였대요

Ex) 어제 만났대요. (= I heard they met yesterday.)

Descriptive Verbs + -았/었/였대요

Ex) 아팠대요. (= I heard she was sick.)

Nouns + -이었/였대요

Ex) 학생이었대요. (= They said they were students.)

Future Tense:

Action Verbs + -(으)ㄹ 거 + 래요

Ex) 내일 만날 거래요. (= He says he will meet them tomorrow.)

Descriptive Verbs + -(으)ㄹ 거 + 래요

Ex) 추울 거래요. (= They say it will be cold.)

Nouns + -일 거 + 래요

Ex) 마지막일 거래요. (= They say it will be the last time.)

Track 33

When you use the -(ㄴ/는)대요/-(이)래요 endings, you usually deliver a piece of information that the other person does not know or that you think they do not know. If you want to emphasize the fact that YOU, at least, have heard something but it might not be the exact truth, you need to use verbs such as "듣다 (= to hear)" and say -다고/라고 들었어요.

Ex)
바쁘다고 들었어요. (= I heard that he is busy.)
어제 만났다고 들었어요. (= I heard that they met yesterday.)
추울 거라고 들었어요. (= I heard that it will be cold.)

Sample Sentences

이게 제일 좋대요.

= They say that this is the best.

여기 정말 유명하대요.

= They say this place is really famous.

몰랐대요.

= He says he did not know.

벌써 다 끝났대요.

= They say it has ended already.

Track 33

어딘지 모른대요.

= He says he does not know where it is.

이 사람 정말 유명한 사람이래요.

= They say this person is a very famous person.

친구가 내일 이사 간대요.

= My friend says she is moving tomorrow.

제 친구가 한국에 올 거래요.

= My friend says he will come to Korea.

　　* If you say, "제 친구가 한국에 올 거라고 했어요", you are saying your friend actually
　　said it him/herself, but by using -래요, you are implying that you may have heard or
　　seen this fact from somewhere else and not your friend.

114

그 사람은 한국에 와 본 적이 없대요.

= He says he has never come to Korea.

주연 씨는 어제도 집에 안 갔대요.

= They say Jooyeon did not go home again yesterday.

Sample Dialogue

경화: 약국에서 주연 씨가 말한 연고
　　　안 판대요.

주연: 저쪽 코너에 있는 약국 갔어요?

경화: 네. 거기는 그 연고 없대요.

주연: 거기 말고 병원 바로 옆에 있는
　　　약국으로 가 보세요. 거기는 팔
　　　거예요.

Kyung-hwa: At the pharmacy, they said that they don't sell the ointment you talked about.

Jooyeon: Did you go to the pharmacy on the corner over there?

Kyung-hwa. Yes. They said that they don't have the ointment.

Jooyeon: Then, go to the pharmacy right next to the hospital, not that one. They should sell it.

Tell Stories, Express Ideas, and

✎ Exercises for Lesson 17

Rewrite the sentences using -(ㄴ/는)대요 *or* -(이)래요 *so you add the meaning of* "They say..." *or* "I hear that..."

1. 이게 제일 좋아요.

→

2. 벌써 다 끝났어요.

→

3. 제 친구가 한국에 올 거예요.

→

4. 이 사람 정말 유명한 사람이에요.

→

5. 그 사람은 한국에 와 본 적이 없어요.

→

Check the answers on **p.201**

LESSON 18

I heard..., They say that...

-(ㄴ/는)다던데(요), -(이)라던데(요)

In the previous lesson, we learned how to say "They say...", or "I hear that..." in Korean in order to re-tell someone what you have heard from someone else. The structures used for saying these are -(ㄴ/는)대(요) and -(이)래(요).

Let us review a little bit.

I.

제 친구가 지금 바빠요. = My friend is busy now.

→ 제 친구가 지금 바쁘대요. = My friend says that she is busy now.

2.

이게 제일 좋은 거예요. = This is the best one.

→ 이게 제일 좋은 거래요. = They say that this is the best one.

Tell Stories, Express Ideas, and

In this lesson, we will look at the following structures:

1. -(ㄴ/는)다던데(요)
2. -(이)라던데(요)

Both of these are very similar to the structures introduced in the previous lesson. -(느)ㄴ다던데(요) is similar to -(ㄴ/는)대(요) (from the first review sentence above) and -(이)라던데(요) is similar to -(이)래(요). Just like -(ㄴ/는)대(요) is an abbreviation of -(ㄴ/는)다고 해(요), -(ㄴ/는)다던데(요) is an abbreviation of -(ㄴ/는)다고 하던데(요). The same applies to -(이)래(요) and -(이)라던데(요).

Difference Between -(ㄴ/는)대(요) and -(ㄴ/는)다던데(요)

Track
35

Whereas -(ㄴ/는)대(요) is used to mainly just retell a story or deliver certain information, when you use -(ㄴ/는)다던데(요), you imply that you want some kind of reaction or response from the listener.

지금 와요. = She is coming now.
지금 온대요. = She says she is coming now.
지금 온다던데요. = She says she is coming now. (+ So should we wait? / What do you think?)

그 사람 유명해요. = He is famous.
그 사람 유명하대요. = They say he is famous.
그 사람 유명하다던데요. = They say he is famous. (+ But you said otherwise, right?)

The same applies to -(이)래(요) and -(이)라던데(요). The only difference is that this follows a noun.

그 사람 학생이에요. = He is a student.

그 사람 학생이래요. = He says he is a student.

그 사람 학생이라던데요. = He says he is a student. (+ So what shall we do then?)

공원이에요. = They are at a park. / It is a park.

공원이래요. = They say they are at a park.

공원이라던데요. = They say they are at a park. (+ Shall we go there?)

Difference Between -(ㄴ/는)다던데(요) and -(ㄴ/는)다는데(요)

There is a slight difference in nuance between -던데 and -는데, and it is based on the fact that -던 is usually associated with the past tense whereas -는 is associated with the present tense. We are going to look at -던 in more detail in a future lesson, so please just note the difference for now.

Track 35

지금 온다던데요. = They said that they would come here now.

지금 온다는데요. = They are saying that they will come here now.

유명하다던데요. = I heard that she is famous.

    * In this case, the person you are talking about is famous now, but you are referring to the fact you heard this in the past.

유명하다는데요. = He is saying that she is famous.

The same applies to -(이)래(요), -(이)라던데(요) and -(이)라는데(요).

학생이라던데요. = They told me that they were students.

학생이라는데요. = They say that they are students.

공원이라던데요. = They said that they were at a park.

공원이라는데요. = They say that they are at a park.

Sample Sentences

여기 위험하다던데요.

= I heard that this place is dangerous. (+ What do you think?)

    * You are implying that the other person should do something or leave the place.

혼자 갈 거라던데요.

= She said she would go there alone. (+ Shall I talk to her again? / You cannot go with her.)

그 사람도 모른다던데요.

= He said that he does not know either. (+ So why keep asking him?)

벌써 다 끝났다던데요.

= They said that it was already all over. (+ There was nothing I could do.)

한국은 겨울에 가면 많이 춥다던데요.

= I heard that it is very cold in Korea if you go there in winter. (+ Perhaps you should pack more clothes.)

Track 35

121

Sample Dialogue

윤기: 이번 학교 축제 때 유명한 가수
　　　온다던데?

호석: 아니야. 가수는 아무도 안 올 거라던데?

윤기: 아무도 안 온다고? 설마.

호석: 진짜야.

Yoongi: I heard that a famous singer is coming to
　　　our upcoming school festival.

Hoseok: No. I heard that no singers would come.

Yoongi: You're saying no singers would come? No
　　　way.

Hoseok: I'm serious.

Tell Stories, Express Ideas, and

✏️ *Exercises for Lesson 18*

Rewrite the sentences that end in -대요/래요 *using* -(ㄴ/는)다던데(요) *or* -(이)라던데(요) *to make them sound like you want a response from the listener.*

1. 지금 온대요.

→

2. 그 사람 유명하대요.

→

3. 그 사람 학생이래요.

→

4. 여기 위험하대요.

→

5. 벌써 다 끝났대요.

→

Check the answers on **p.201**

123

LESSON 19

Making Reported Question Sentences

-냐고

In this lesson, let us take a look at how to report questions in Korean. Reported questions are questions within sentences such as, "I asked him when he was going to finish his work", "He asked me how old I was", etc. In writing, you can quote the actual questions word for word, but when you speak with others, it is more natural to form reported question sentences. Let us learn how to do that in Korean.

To make a reported question sentence, you use the ending **-냐고** and add a question-related word.

> ### Conjugation
> Verb stem + **-냐고** + Question related word

Examples of Question Related Words
1. 묻다 = to ask
2. 물어보다 = to ask

3. 말하다 = to say

4. 질문하다 = to ask a question

Examples of Reported Questions

(1)

학생이에요?

= Are you a student?

→ 학생 + -이 (verb stem)* + -냐고

→ 학생이냐고

→ 학생이냐고 물어봤어요.

= They asked me if I was a student. / I asked her if she was a student.

* After a noun, you need to add 이다 (= to be) to make it a verb.

(2)

뭐예요?

= What is it?

→ 뭐 + -이 (verb stem) + -냐고

→ 뭐(이)냐고* → 뭐냐고

→ 뭐냐고 물어봤어요.

= She asked what this is. / I asked what it is. / They asked what that is.

* When a noun ends with a vowel and without a last consonant, you can omit -이. For example, 누구 is followed by 이다, but when also followed by -냐고, it changes to 누구냐고 instead of 누구이냐고.

(3)
누가 그렇게 말했어요?
= Who said so?

→ 누가 + 그렇게 + 말하 (verb stem) + -았/었/였 (past tense suffix) + -냐고

→ 누가 그렇게 말했냐고

→ 누가 그렇게 말했냐고 물었어요.
= I asked who said so. / They asked who said such a thing.

Track
37

Sample Sentences

몇 시에 올 거냐고 물어보세요.
= Ask him what time he will come here.

왜 안 왔냐고 물어봤는데, 대답을 안 해요.
= I asked him why he did not come here, but he will not answer.

저한테 어디 가냐고 물었어요.
= He asked me where I was going.

저는 몇 살이냐고 물어보는 게 제일 싫어요.
= I hate it the most when people ask me how old I am.

몇 살이냐고 물어봤어요.

= (Someone) asked me how old I was.

저도 가야 되냐고 물어봐 주세요.

= Please ask them if I have to come along, too.

Track 37

Sample Dialogue

Track 38

에밀리: 한국 사람들은 왜 항상 밥 먹었냐고
물어봐요?

캐시: 한국 사람들한테는 그게 인사예요.

에밀리: 밥 말고 다른 거 먹었으면 뭐라고
말해요?

캐시: 그냥 먹었다고 하면 돼요. 뭐 먹었냐고
물어보는 거 아니에요.

*Emily: Why do Korean people always ask if you
have eaten rice?*

Cassie: To Korean people, that is a greeting.

*Emily: If I had something else rather than rice,
what should I say?*

*Cassie: You can just say you have eaten. It's not
that they're asking what you ate.*

✎ Exercises for Lesson 19

Make reported question sentences by combining two sentences.

Check the answers on **p.201**

1.

"몇 시에 올 거예요?"
이렇게 물어보세요.   →

2.

"학생이에요?"
이렇게 물어봤어요.   →

3.

"몇 살이에요?"
이렇게 물어봤어요.   →

4.

"어디 가요?"
저한테 이렇게 말했어요.   →

5.

"저도 가야 돼요?"
이렇게 물어봐 주세요.   →

LESSON **20**

Sentence Building Drill 10

Sentence Building Drill 10

In this series, we focus on how you can use the grammatical rules and expressions that you have learned so far to train yourself to comfortably and flexibly make more Korean sentences.

We will start off with THREE key sentences, then practice changing parts of these sentences so that you do not end up just memorizing the same three sentences. We want you to be able to be as flexible as possible with the Korean sentences that you can make.

Key Sentence (1)

어제 주연 씨를 만났는데, 머리를 빨간 색으로 염색했더라고요.

= I met Jooyeon yesterday and you know what, I saw that she had dyed her hair red.

Key Sentence (2)

경화 씨는 일 끝난 다음에 친구 만난대요.

= Kyung-hwa says she is going to meet her friends after she finishes work.

130

Key Sentence (3)

아무리 피곤해도 지금 자면 안 돼요.

= No matter how tired you are, you should not sleep now.

Expansion & Variation Practice with Key Sentence (1)

0. Original Sentence:

어제 주연 씨를 만났는데, 머리를 빨간색으로 염색했더라고요.

= I met Jooyeon yesterday, and you know what, I saw that she had dyed her hair red.

Track
39

1.

어제 주연 씨를 만났는데

= I met Jooyeon yesterday, and you know what...

어제 친구들이랑 영화를 봤는데

= I saw a movie with my friends yesterday, and you know what...

저도 그 책 읽었는데

= I read that book too, and you know what...

석진 씨한테 물어봤는데

= I asked Seokjin, and you know what...

집에 가서 냉장고 문을 열었는데

= I went home and opened the refrigerator door, and you know what...

2.

머리를 빨간색으로 염색했더라고요.

= I saw that she had dyed her hair red.

사람이 정말 많더라고요.

= (I saw that) there were so many people there.

이게 제일 좋더라고요.

= (I know from my experience that) this one is the best.

정말 재미있더라고요.

= I found it a lot of fun.

생각보다 어렵더라고요.

= I found it more difficult than I had thought.

* -더라고요 is retelling or reporting on speech.

Expansion & Variation Practice with Key Sentence (2)

0. Original Sentence:

경화 씨는 일 끝난 다음에 친구 만난대요.

= Kyung-hwa says she is going to meet her friends after she finishes work.

Track 39

1.

일 끝난 다음에 = after work finishes

책 다 읽은 다음에 = after you finish reading the book

영화 본 다음에 = after we watch the movie

이메일 답장 한 다음에 = after I reply to the email

집에 간 다음에 = after you go home

2.

친구 만난대요. = She says that she is going to meet a friend.

오늘 서울은 날씨가 춥대요. = I hear that the weather is cold in Seoul today.

경화 씨가 오늘 주연 씨 만날 거래요. = Kyung-hwa says that she will meet Jooyeon today.

여기 스파게티 정말 맛있대요. = I hear that the spaghetti here is really delicious.

윤아 씨 오늘 바쁘대요. = Yoona says that she is busy today.

Expansion & Variation Practice with Key Sentence (3)

0. Original Sentence:

아무리 피곤해도 지금 자면 안 돼요.

= No matter how tired you are, you should not sleep now.

1.

아무리 피곤해도 = No matter how tired you are...

아무리 어려워도 = No matter how difficult it is...

아무리 화가 나도 = No matter how upset you are...

날씨가 아무리 추워도 = No matter how cold the weather is...

책을 아무리 많이 읽어도 = No matter how many books you read...

2.

Track 39

지금 자면 안 돼요 = You should not sleep now.

이거 잃어버리면 안 돼요 = You should not lose it.

혼자 가면 안 돼요 = You should not go there alone.

늦으면 안 돼요 = You should not be late.

커피 너무 많이 마시면 안 돼요 = You should not drink too much coffee.

133

Sample Dialogue

Track 40

경은: 경화 씨, 주연 씨한테 전화해 보세요.

경화: 아까 전화했는데 안 받더라고요.

경은: 그래요? 다시 한 번 해 보세요.

경화: 네. (잠시 후) 아무리 해도 안 받아요.

Kyeong-eun: Kyung-hwa, try calling Jooyeon.

Kyung-hwa: I called her earlier, but she didn't answer.

Kyeong-eun: She didn't? Please try calling her again.

Kyung-hwa: Okay. (a little later) No matter how many times I do, she doesn't answer.

✎ Exercises for Lesson **20**

Translate each phrase or sentence into Korean and write it on the lines provided.

1. No matter how difficult it is...

....

2. After we watch the movie...

....

3. You should not sleep now.

....

4. I hear that the weather is cold in Seoul today.

....

5. I found it more difficult than I had thought.

....

Check the answers on **p.202**

135

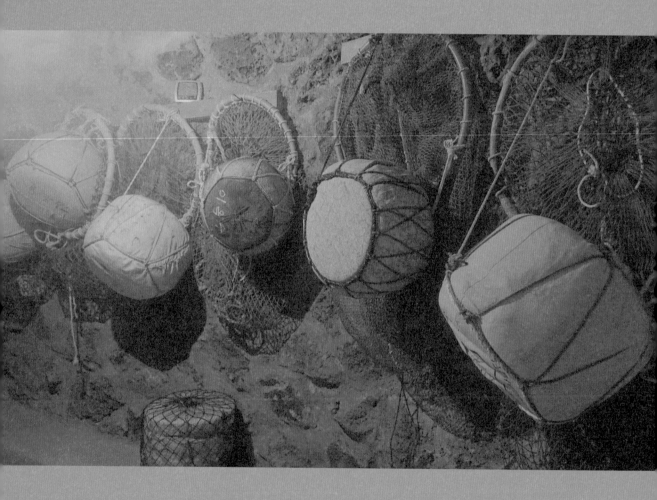

Female Free Divers on Jeju Island
(해녀)

Jeju Island is known to have an abundance of three things. Due to this, it was given the name Samdado (삼: three, 다: a lot, 도: island). The three things it is said to have an abundance of are wind, stone, and women. It is the third which I will discuss in this blog: Jeju Women.

Jeju is thought to be an island of goddesses. Most of the deities of Jeju are women and they tell the legend of how Jeju Island came to be. If you do not remember, we talked about that in Book 6; Seolmundae (설문대) created Jeju Island when sand fell through holes in her skirt. But what I really want to jump into today is the women of Jeju, and to be more specific, the haenyeo (해녀).

Haenyeo are female divers that reside on Jeju Island. You can typically see them swimming in the ocean with their distinct black wetsuits, circular goggles, and big nets to carry that day's catch. Or, while traveling down the coast, you might see an orange or yellow flotation device floating in the water. This means the haenyeo are hard at work diving to the bottom of the ocean to catch their earnings.

Let us start with a little background on the haenyeo. In Seoul, men were the main source of household income and women would typically stay at home to take care of the children and the house. However, in Jeju, women were the main source of income and these women were often divers. Not only were these women important to their own families, but they were also important for economic growth in Jeju. They even pioneered trade by traveling to nearby countries with their gatherings from the ocean.

They were also a huge influence in their own communities. In one town, the haenyeo helped pave roads and even built a school by donating part of their income. There was once something called a "school badang" (학교바당) that supplied fees to elementary schools. Then in 1950, a local school burnt down, so the haenyeo contributed money to the rebuilding of the school by selling seaweed they gathered from the ocean.

As you can see, the haenyeo were and still are quite important to society on Jeju Island. Now, I would like to tell you about some of the things you might see or hear when you are near the haenyeo. For one, there is something called "sumbisori" (숨비소리), which is the whistling sound the haenyeo make when they surface the water. The sound comes from the divers inhaling oxygen and exhaling carbon dioxide built up from their dive that can last up to 2 minutes. This is said to allow them to work for extended periods of time with very short breaks.

Today, the haenyeo mostly wear black wetsuits while diving into the ocean. The wetsuits protect them from cold temperatures, allow them to spend more time in the water, and even allow them to be more efficient while underneath the surface. The wetsuit typically consists of pants, a top, water socks, a cap for their head, and fins. However, before wetsuits were created, they used swimsuits that were made out of cotton. It would consist of a top, bottom, and a towel to hold their hair. They could only spend about an hour in the water during the winter months and then would spend 3 to 4 hours by a fire to warm up before jumping back into the water. Now, they can spend up to 6 hours at a time in the water. Along with their wetsuits, the haenyeo use tools to make it easier to collect octopus, oysters, sea urchins, abalone, as well as many other things that reside on the bottom of the ocean. One item that you will see floating on the surface is called a "taewak" (테왁망사리), which are nets attached to a buoy for the haenyeo to store the items they catch. The masks they wear are called "nun" (왕눈), and are oval shaped with a leather strap to go around their head.

The more I learn about the haenyeo, the more I understand their importance to Jeju. A lot of these women started diving when they were 7 or 8 years old and have been doing it ever since. Some are now in their 80's and are still diving! If you are ever in Jeju, I would highly suggest checking out the Haenyeo Museum. It is not a big museum but you can learn a lot about the history of the haenyeo. When you first walk in, there is a theater that shows a quick video introducing the haenyeo. They have Korean and English versions available as well. Afterwards, you can walk at your own pace through the rest of the museum. I suggest making your way to the observatory to get a fantastic view of the ocean.

There is even a Jeju Haenyeo Festival which is the nation's only women-centered maritime festival. It not only celebrates the haenyeo but also helps to preserve the traditional culture of the women of Jeju Island. There are also several places around the island where you can participate in a haenyeo experience. They teach you the technique of diving without an oxygen tank and how to gather food from the bottom of the ocean.

Written by Johnny Bland

LESSON **21**

Didn't you hear them say...

-(ㄴ/는)다잖아요/라잖아요

Track
41

For the past few lessons, we have been looking at the various ways to make reported speech sentences. In this lesson, let us take a look at the verb endings -(ㄴ/는)다잖아요 and -라잖아요. We introduced a similar ending, -잖아요, in Level 5 Lesson 27, which is used to express "Don't you see that...", "Come on, isn't it...", etc. By adding the -(ㄴ/는)다 or -라 before -잖아요, you can add a "reported speech" function to it, such as "Don't you see this person is saying..." or "Don't you hear me saying...".

Review of -잖아요

l. 석진 씨 지금 여기 없어요. = Seokjin is not here now.

→ 석진 씨 지금 여기 없잖아요. = Don't you see that Seokjin is not here now?

2. 오늘 일요일이에요. = Today is Sunday.

→ 오늘 일요일이잖아요. = Come on, it is Sunday.

Usage of -(ㄴ/는)다잖아요 and -라잖아요

The construction is the same as other structures that use -(ㄴ/는)다 or -라. In the present tense, you add -ㄴ/는다 for action verbs and just -다 with adjectives/descriptive verbs. With nouns, you add -이 from 이다 and add -라.

The meaning of this structure is a combination of -(ㄴ/는)다고/라고 (reported speech, quotation) and -잖아요. Therefore, you can use this structure when you want to say "Don't you see that..." or "Come on..." while quoting someone.

Examples

(1)

좋아요. = It is good.

좋잖아요. = Come on, it is good. / Isn't it good?

좋다잖아요. = Come on, they say it is good. / Come on, they say they like it.

(2)

여기 없어요. = He is not here.

여기 없잖아요. = Don't you see he is not here?

여기 없다잖아요. = Don't you hear them say he is not here? / Didn't you hear them say he is not here?

(3)

혼자 가요. = I go there by myself.

혼자 가잖아요. = You know I go there alone.

혼자 간다잖아요. = Don't you hear me saying that I am going there alone? / Didn't you hear me saying that I am going there alone?

(4)

친구 만날 거예요. = He will meet a friend.

친구 만날 거잖아요. = You know he will meet a friend.

친구 만날 거라잖아요. = Come on, he says he will meet a friend.

* 만날 거 is actually a noun group due to the -거.

Sample Sentences

싫다잖아요. 하지 마세요.

= She says she does not like it. Do not do it.

주연 씨 지금 바쁘다잖아요.

= Come on, Jooyeon says she is busy now.

= Don't you hear Jooyeon saying she is busy now?

Track 41

실수였다잖아요. 용서해 줘요.

= He says it was a mistake. Forgive him.

아니라잖아요. 왜 그 사람 말을 안 믿어요?

= Don't you hear him saying it is not true? Why do you not believe what he says?

맞다잖아요!

= You see? He says it is true!

Sample Dialogue

Track
42

현우: 캐시 씨, 점심 같이 먹을래요?

캐시: 아니요. 저는 혼자 먹을게요.

현우: 같이 먹어요.

경은: 캐시 씨가 혼자 먹겠다잖아요. 현우 씨랑 같이 먹기 싫다잖아요.

Hyunwoo: Cassie, do you want to have lunch with us?

Cassie: No. I will eat on my own.

Hyunwoo: Let's have lunch together.

Kyeong-eun: Didn't you hear Cassie say she will eat by herself? Come on, she said that she doesn't want to eat with you!

144

Tell Stories, Express Ideas, and

✏ Exercises for Lesson 21

Fill in the blanks by using -(ㄴ/는)다잖아요 *or* -라잖아요.

1. (   ). 하지 마세요.

   = She says she does not like it. Do not do it.

2. 주연 씨 지금 (   )

   = Come on, Jooyeon says she is busy now.

   = Don't you hear Jooyeon saying she is busy now?

3. (   ). 용서해 줘요.

   = He says it was a mistake. Forgive him.

4. (   ). 왜 그 사람 말을 안 믿어요?

   = Don't you hear him saying it is not true? Why do you not believe what he says?

5. (   )!

   = You see? He says it is true!

Check the answers on **p.202**

LESSON 22

Word Builder 14

정(定)

Track 43

Word Builder lessons are designed to help you understand how to expand your vocabulary by learning and understanding some common and basic building blocks of Korean words. The words and letters introduced through Word Builder lessons are not necessarily all Chinese characters, or 한자. Though many of them are based on Chinese characters, the meanings can be different from modern-day Chinese. Your goal through these lessons is to understand how words are formed and then remember the keywords in Korean to expand your Korean vocabulary from there. You certainly do not have to memorize the Hanja characters, but if you want to, feel free!

Today's key word element is 정.

The Chinese character for this is 定.
There are many other Chinese characters (or Hanja) for 정, so keep in mind that not all the words that have 정 in them have related meanings.

146

The word 정 (定) is related to "to decide", "to choose", or "to correct".

결 (to decide) + 정 (to decide) = 결정 決定 = decision

인 (to recognize) + 정 (to decide) = 인정 認定 = admitting, approval

Ex)

인정을 하다

= to approve, to admit (that one has done something)

인정을 받다

= (someone's achievement) is recognized or (someone's status/position) is approved

예 (in advance) + 정 (to decide) = 예정 豫定 = scheduling, planning

확 (to harden, to solidify) + 정 (to decide) = 확정 確定 = confirmation, finalization

Track 43

일 (one) + 정 (to decide) = 일정 一定 = fixed, regular, constant

* The adjective form is 일정한.

** This 일정 is different from 일정 (日程), which means schedule.

Ex)

일정한 시간에 = at a fixed time

속도가 일정하다 = the speed is constant

가격이 일정하다 = the price is constant

특 (special, particular) + 정 (to choose) = 특정 特定 = particular, specific

판 (to judge) + 정 (to decide) = 판정 判定 = judgment, decision

* This word is almost always used during matches or games that require a judge or referee.

Ex)

판정이 나다 = to give a judgment

판정을 내리다 = to make a judgment

판정승 = win by point count (compared to a win by knockout)

설 (set) + 정 (to decide) = 설정 設定 = setting, set-up

가 (fake) + 정 (to decide) = 가정 假定 = supposition, assumption

정 (to decide) + 원 (member) = 정원 定員 = fixed member, capacity

안 (comfortable) + 정 (to decide) = 안정 安定 = stability, calm

Ex)

안정을 취하다 = to get some rest, to stabilize oneself

정 (to decide) + 기 (period) = 정기 定期 = periodical, regular

Ex)

정기 구독 = regular subscription, periodical subscription

정 (to decide) + 식 (manner, method) = 정식 定式 = formal, legal

Ex)

정식으로 = in a formal manner, officially, legally

정식으로 인사 드릴게요. = Let me officially introduce myself.

정 (to decide) + 가 (price) = 정가 定價 = fixed price, official price

고 (to solidify, to harden) + 정 (to choose) = 고정 固定 = fixation, fastening

Track 43

Sample Dialogue

경화: 어떤 옷 살 거예요?

석진: 아직 결정 못 했어요.

경화: 이 옷은 정가가 십만 원인데 팔십 프로 세일해서 이만 원이래요.

석진: 우와! 저 그 옷 살래요.

Kyung-hwa: Which clothes are you going to buy?

Seokjin: I haven't decided yet.

Kyung-hwa: It says that the official price of these clothes is 100,000 won, but they are 80% off, so they are 20,000 won.

Seokjin: Wow! I will buy those clothes.

✏ Exercises for Lesson **22**

Fill in the blanks with the appropriate Sino-Korean word from the lesson.

1. The key word element (   ) is related to "to decide", "to choose", or "to correct".

2. (   ) = decision

3. (   ) = fixed price, official price

4. (   ) = fixation, fastening

5. (   ) = scheduling, planning

Check the answers on **p.202**

151

LESSON **23**

No matter whether you do it or not

-(으)나 마나

Track
45

In this lesson, let us take a look at how to say "no matter whether" someone does something or not. The verb ending you can use to say this in Korean is **-(으)나 마나**. This is very similar to -아/어/여 봤자 (Level 7 Lesson 7), but the difference is that -아/어/여 봤자 has a stronger nuance of, "Even if you go ahead and do it, you will not achieve what you want", whereas -(으)나 마나 is closer to, "No matter whether you do it or not, the result is fixed."

| *Conjugation*
| Verb stem + -(으)나 마나

Ex)

먹다 → 먹 + -으나 마나 = 먹으나 마나

보다 → 보 + -나 마나 = 보나 마나

* 마나 comes from the verb, 말다.

보나 마나, 이상할 거예요.

= No matter whether you see it or not, (I am sure) it will be strange.

= You do not even have to see it. It will be strange.

Sometimes, -(으)나 마나 is followed by the -이다 verb in the form of -(으)나 마나예요.

보나 마나예요.

= You do not even have to look at it. What you will see is fixed. I know what you will see.

= I do not even have to bother looking at it. I know what I will see.

Sample Sentences

물어보나 마나 안 된다고 할 거예요.

= Whether you ask them or not, they will certainly say no.

Track
45

하나 마나 똑같아요.

= No matter whether you do it or not, the result is the same.

이야기를 하나 마나 하나도 달라지는 게 없어요.

= No matter whether you talk to him or not, nothing changes.

   * If the other person can sense what you are going to say, you can just say it in the shorter form, "이야기를 하나 마나예요."

보나 마나 제가 일등이에요.

= No need to see. I am the 1st place winner.

이 책은 읽으나 마나예요.

= This book is worthless to read.

Sample Dialogue

석진: 우리 볼링 시합할까요?

경은: 보나 마나 주연 씨가 일등 하겠죠.

석진: 안 그럴 수도 있죠. 내기해요.

경은: 보나 마나예요.

Seokjin: Shall we have a bowling match?

Kyeong-eun: We don't have to. Jooyeon will be the
winner.

Seokjin: She might not be, right? Let's make a bet.

Kyeong-eun: No need to.

Tell Stories, Express Ideas, and

✏️ Exercises for Lesson 23

Fill in the blanks by using -(으)나 마나.

1. (⟩ 안 된다고 할 거예요.

   = Whether you ask them or not, they will certainly say no.

2. (⟩ 똑같아요.

   = No matter whether you do it or not, the result is the same.

3. (⟩ 하나도 달라지는 게 없어요.

   = No matter whether you talk to him or not, nothing changes.

4. (⟩ 제가 일등이에요.

   = No need to see. I am the 1st place winner.

5. 이 책은 ( )예요.

   = This book is worthless to read.

Check the answers on **p.202**

LESSON 24

To have been put into a certain state

Passive Voice + -어 있다

In Level 6 Lesson 21 and 23, we looked at how the passive voice works in Korean. In this lesson, let us learn a structure that you can use with the passive voice to say that something has been put into a certain state and stays that way.

For example, the verb for "to put something somewhere" is 놓다. The passive voice is 놓이다, so you can say, "놓였어요" to mean, "It was put down (on the table/ground/etc. and it remains there)."

You can use this grammatical structure when you want to say that something is on the floor/table/etc. because it has been put down there by someone.

Passive Voice + -어 있다

= to have been put into a certain state (by someone) and stay that way

156

What is the difference between "Passive Voice" and "Passive Voice + -어 있다"?

Passive voice describes an action as it gets done, whereas "Passive voice + -어 있다" expresses the state that the subject is in as a result of the passive action. This "resultant state" structure is more commonly used in Korean than in English; for phrases that you want to express in English with just the passive voice, you can use this structure to express it instead.

Examples

(1)
잡다 = to catch
잡히다 = to be caught
잡혀 있다 = to be in custody, to have been caught (and is still caught now)

Track 47

(2)
깨다 = to break
깨지다 = to be broken, to be shattered
깨져 있다 = to be in a broken state, somebody broke it (and it is still in that state)

(3)
켜다 = to turn on, to switch on
켜지다 = to be turned on, to be switched on
켜져 있다 = somebody turned it on (and it is still on)

(4)
쌓다 = to pile things up
쌓이다 = to be piled up

157

쌓여 있다 = to have been piled up (ex: snow)

(5)

열다 = to open

열리다 = to be opened

열려 있다 = to have been opened (and stay open)

* Note that you cannot use this structure with transitive verbs.

Sample Sentences

문이 열려 있어요.

= The door is open!

Track 47

에어컨이 아직 켜져 있어요.

= The air conditioning is still on.

여기 사과가 한 개 놓여 있어요.

= Somebody put an apple here.

= Here's an apple.

    * The difference between, "여기 사과가 한 개 있어요" and "여기 사과가 한 개 놓여 있어요" is that with the second phrase, you are sure that someone placed it there.

이 마을은 산으로 둘러쌓여 있어요.

= This town is surrounded by mountains.

파란색으로 칠해져 있는 간판 보여요?

= Do you see the sign there that is painted in blue?

158

아침에 일어나니까 눈이 쌓여 있었어요.

= When I woke up this morning, I saw that the snow had been piled up.

제가 깬 거 아니에요. 깨져 있었어요.

= I did not break it. It was broken when I saw it.

Track 47

159

Sample Dialogue

경은: 오늘 점심 어디서 먹을까요?

석진: 라면집 옆에 있는 파스타집 갈까요?

경은: 거기는 점심때 문을 안 여나 봐요. 항상 닫혀 있더라고요.

석진: 그래요? 어제 점심 시간에는 열려 있었어요. 한번 가 봐요.

Kyeong-eun: Where shall we have lunch today?

Seokjin: Shall we go to the pasta place next to the ramyeon place?

Kyeong-eun: I guess that place is not open for lunch. From what I've seen it's always closed.

Seokjin: Is that so? It was open at lunchtime yesterday. Let's check it out.

Tell Stories, Express Ideas, and

✐ Exercises for Lesson **24**

Translate the following words and phrases into Korean.

1.

to catch →

to be caught →

to be in custody, to have been caught (and is still caught now) →

2.

to break →

to be broken, to be shattered →

to be in a broken state, somebody broke it (and it is still in that state) →

3

to turn on, to switch on →

to be turned on, to be switched on →

somebody turned it on (and it is still on) →

4.

to pile things up →

to be piled up →

to have been piled up (ex: snow) →

5.

to open →

to be opened →

to have been opened (and stay open) →

Check the answers on **p.202**

161

LESSON 25

To be bound to + verb

동사 + -게 되어 있다

Track
49

In the previous lesson (Level 7 Lesson 24), we looked at how you can combine the passive voice form with -어 있다 to express a "resultant state". In this lesson, we will look at a similar, yet fixed structure, using the verb 되다.

되다 = to become, to be done

되다 can mean "to become", but it can also work as the passive voice of the verb 하다 and mean "to be done".

-게 되다 = to get to do something, to gradually do something

-게 되다 (Level 4 Lesson 29) expresses how someone or something happens, comes to be, or becomes a certain state.

-게 되어 있다 = to be destined to do something, to be bound to be in a certain state

162

"Passive Voice + -어 있다" expresses a "resultant state" of things; therefore when you say -게 되어 있다, you mean that something is "bound" to be in a certain state, or "destined" to happen in a certain way.

Examples

(1)
알다 = to know
알게 되다 = to get to know
알게 되어 있다 = to be in a situation where you are bound to know or find out

(2)
보이다 = to be seen
보이게 되다 = to become visible
보이게 되어 있다 = cannot help but be visible

Track
49

(3)
하다 = to do
하게 되다 = to get to do
하게 되어 있다 = to be bound to do, to have no other choice but to do

Sample Sentences

공부는 정말 필요하면 열심히 하게 되어 있어요.

= As for studying, if it is really necessary, you are bound to study hard.

아무리 게을러도, 손님이 오면 집 청소를 하게 되어 있어요.

= No matter how lazy you are, you are bound to clean the house when a guest comes.

아무리 바빠도, 데이트 시간은 생기게 되어 있어요.

= No matter how busy you are, you somehow always find time for dating.

영원한 비밀은 없어요. 사람들이 알게 되어 있어요.

= There is no eternal secret. People will eventually find out.

재미있게 공부하면 성적도 좋아지게 되어 있어요.

= If you have fun while studying, your grades are bound to get better.

Track 49

Tell Stories, Express Ideas, and

Sample Dialogue

Track 50

석진: 저는 글은 잘 쓰는데, 말은 잘
　　 못하는 것 같아요.

현우: 아니에요. 글을 잘 쓰면 말도
　　 잘하게 되어 있어요.

석진: 그냥 많이 하면 잘하게 될까요?

현우: 네. 연습을 많이 하면 늘게 되어
　　 있어요.

*Seokjin: I am good at writing, but I don't think I am
　　 good at speaking.*

*Hyunwoo: That's not true. If you are good at writing,
　　 you are bound to be good at speaking as well.*

*Seokjin: I wonder if I am bound to get better at it if I
　　 do it a lot?*

*Hyunwoo: I think so. You are bound to get better if you
　　 practice a lot.*

✏ Exercises for Lesson 25

Check the answers on **p.202**

Fill in the blanks by using -게 되어 있다.

1. 영원한 비밀은 없어요. ( ).

= There is no eternal secret. People will eventually find out.

2. 공부는 정말 필요하면 ( ).

= As for studying, if it is really necessary, you are bound to study hard.

3. 재미있게 공부하면 성적도 ( ).

= If you have fun while studying, your grades are bound to get better.

4. 아무리 바빠도, 데이트 시간은 ( ).

= No matter how busy you are, you somehow always find time for dating.

5. 아무리 게을러도, 손님이 오면 ( ).

= No matter how lazy you are, you are bound to clean the house when a guest comes.

LESSON **26**

On top of…, In addition to…

-(으/느)ㄴ 데다가

In this lesson, let us take a look at how to say "in addition to ＋ Verb-ing" or "on top of ＋ Verb-ing" in Korean. The structure for this is -(으/느)ㄴ 데다가.

Track 51

How It Is Formed

데 by itself means "a place" or "a spot", but it is always attached to another Korean word, like in 아픈 데, which means a place that hurts (on your body).

> **Ex)** 좋은 데 데려가 줄게요. ＝ I will take you to a good place.

-다가 means "adding to this" or "to this place" as in, "Put it over here (＝ 여기에다가 놓으세요)" or, "I left it at home (＝ 집에다가 두고 왔어요)" You could also just say, "여기에 놓으세요" or "집에 두고 왔어요", but by using -다가, it adds more direction to the meaning.

By adding 데 to -다가, you form 데다가, which means "on the place of…" or "adding to the spot where…".

167

When you add -(으/느)ㄴ, you can connect other verbs to 데다가.

All together, -(으/느)ㄴ 데다가 means "on top of..." or "in addition to..."

Track 51

Conjugation

Present tense:

Action verb + -는 데다가

Ex) 먹다 → 먹는 데다가

Descriptive verb + -(으)ㄴ 데다가

Ex) 예쁘다 → 예쁜 데다가

Past tense:

Verb stem + -(으)ㄴ 데다가

Ex) 먹다 → 먹은 데다가

Examples

(1)
예쁘다 = to be pretty
예쁜 데다가 = in addition to being pretty

(2)
바쁘다 = to be busy
바쁜 데다가 = in addition to being busy

(3)

비싸다 = to be expensive

비싼 데다가 = in addition to being expensive

When using -(으/느)ㄴ 데다가 in a sentence, it is usually followed by a clause that is consistent with the previous phrase. Therefore, the two clauses in the sentence should be consistent with each other. -도 (also) is often used in the second clause as well.

Sample Sentences

석진 씨는 잘생긴 데다가 키도 커요.

= In addition to being handsome, Seokjin is also tall.

Track 51

주연 씨는 똑똑한 데다가 공부도 열심히 해요.

= In addition to being smart, Jooyeon studies hard too.

경은 씨는 예쁜 데다가 성격도 좋아요.

= In addition to being pretty, Kyeong-eun also has a nice personality.

이 식당은 시끄러운 데다가 맛도 없어요.

= In addition to being noisy, this restaurant's food is also not good.

경화 씨는 친구가 많은 데다가 하는 일도 많아서 만나기 어려워요.

= In addition to having a lot of friends, Kyung-hwa also does lots of things, so it is difficult to meet her.

   * You could simplify this by saying, "경화 씨는 친구가 많아요. 그리고 하는 일도 많아요. 그래서 만나기 어려워요" but it is better to combine them all into one sentence.

Sample Dialogue

Track 52

주인: 어서 오세요.

손님: 안녕하세요.

주인: 여기가 좁은 골목에 있는 데다가
  간판도 없어서 찾아오기 힘드셨죠?

손님: 네. 제가 길치인데다가 홍대를 처음
  와서 찾기 어렵더라고요.

Owner: Welcome.

Guest: Hello.

*Owner: On top of being in a narrow alleyway, we
also don't have a sign, so you must have
had a hard time finding us, right?*

*Guest: Yes. In addition to not being good with
roads, this is my first time coming to
Hongdae, so it was hard to find.*

✎ *Exercises for Lesson* **26**

Fill in the blanks by using -(으/느)ㄴ 데다가.

I. 석진 씨는 ( ) 키도 커요.

   = In addition to being handsome, Seokjin is also tall.

2. 주연 씨는 ( ) 공부도 열심히 해요.

   = In addition to being smart, Jooyeon studies hard too.

3. 경은 씨는 ( ) 성격도 좋아요.

   = In addition to being pretty, Kyeong-eun also has a nice personality.

4. 이 식당은 ( ) 맛도 없어요.

   = In addition to being noisy, this restaurant's food is also not good.

5. 경화 씨는 친구가 ( ) 하는 일도 많아서 만나기 어려워요.

   = In addition to having a lot of friends, Kyung-hwa also does lots of things, so it is difficult to meet her.

LESSON 27

As long as

-기만 하면, -(느)ㄴ 한

Track 53

In this lesson, let us take a look at how to say "as long as" in Korean. This is not the literal comparison of two things as in, "A is as long as B", but a fixed expression "as long as + Subject + Verb" as in, "As long as you stay here, you are safe." Let us find out how to say this in Korean!

How to Say "As Long As" in Korean

There are a few ways to say this in Korean.

I. Verb stem + **-기만 하면**

(Original literal translation = "if + Subject + only + Verb")

> **Ex)**
> 여기에 있기만 하면 괜찮아요.
> = As long you are here, you are fine.
> You could also say, "여기에 있기만 하면 돼요."

Tell Stories, Express Ideas, and

재미있게 공부하기만 하면, 한국어 잘할 수 있어요.

= As long as you study Korean in a fun way, you can become good at Korean.

2. Verb stem + -(느)ㄴ 한

(Original literal translation = "within the boundaries where Subject + Verb")

* This form is a little more formal than the other forms, so you wouldn't really use it in spoken language. You will see it more in written language.

Ex)

제가 열쇠를 가지고 있는 한, 아무도 못 들어가요.

= As long as I have the keys, no one can go in.

3. Verb stem + -지만 않으면

(Original literal translation = "only if + Subject + does not + Verb")

-지 않다 is the negative form of a neutral Korean sentence.

Ex)

너무 춥지만 않으면 갈게요.

= As long as it is not too cold, I will go/come.

너무 덥지만 않으면 갈게요.

= As long as it is not too hot, I will go/come.

Sample Sentences

비밀을 지키기만 하면 안전해요.

= As long as you keep the secret, you are safe.

사람들이 너무 많이 오지만 않으면 괜찮아요.

= As long as not too many people come here, it is okay.

깨지지만 않으면, 계속 쓸 수 있어요.

= As long as it is not broken, you can keep using it.

살아있는 한, 저는 계속 공부를 할 거예요.

= As long as I am alive, I will keep studying.

음식이 맛있고 직원이 친절하기만 하면, 식당은 언젠가 유명해져요.

= As long as the food is good and the staff are kind, the restaurant will become famous one day.

> * Note that there are two verbs being used here, but we only add -기만 하면 to the second verb.

Track 53

Sample Dialogue

Track
54

주인: 잘 데가 이 소파밖에 없는데
　　　어떡하죠?

손님: 괜찮아요. 저는 아무 데나 눕기만
　　　하면 자요.

주인: 불편할 것 같아서요.

손님: 괜찮다니까요. 너무 춥지만 않으면
　　　푹 잘 수 있어요. 여기 춥지는 않죠?

주인: 네. 창문을 열고 자지 않는 한 안
　　　추울 거예요.

Owner: There's nowhere but this sofa to sleep.
　　　　What should we do?

Guest: It's fine. I can sleep anywhere as long as
　　　　I can lie down.

Owner: (I'm worried because) I think it will be
　　　　uncomfortable.

Guest: I said it's fine. As long as it is not too cold,
　　　　I can sleep well. It's not too cold here, right?

Owner: No. As long as you don't sleep with the
　　　　window open, it is not going to be cold.

175

Check the answers on **p.203**

✏ Exercises for Lesson **27**

Rewrite the sentences using -(느)ㄴ 한 in order to make it sound more formal.

1. 비밀을 지키기만 하면 안전해요. →

2. 깨지지만 않으면, 계속 쓸 수 있어요. →

3. 여기에 있기만 하면 괜찮아요. →

4. 사람들이 너무 많이 오지만 않으면 괜찮아요. →

5. 너무 춥지만 않으면 갈게요. →

176

LESSON **28**

The thing that is called + verb

-(ㄴ/는)다는 것

In Level 6 Lesson 15, we looked at the structure -(이)라는 것, which is used to express what you think is the definition or the nature of something. You can do the same with verbs, except with a slightly different structure.

Track 55

Let us review a little bit first.

Noun + -(이)라는 것
= What I call "Noun" is...
= (I think that) "Noun" is...

> **Ex)**
> 평화라는 것은...
> = (I think that) Peace is...
>
> 우정이라는 것은...
> = (In my opinion, the nature of) Friendship is...

In order to express the same thing with verbs, you need to use the structure, -(ㄴ/는)다는 것.

Verb stem + -(ㄴ/는)다는 것

-(ㄴ/는)다는 것 originally comes from -(ㄴ/는)다고 하는 것, which means "the thing that is called + Verb" and it is used to express what you think is the definition or the nature of a certain action/state/verb.

Ex)
배우다 = to learn
배우 + -ㄴ다는 것 → 배운다는 것 = the act of learning
배운다는 것은 언제나 즐거운 일이에요. = Learning is always a pleasant thing to do.
* By using this form, it implies that you are talking about the nature/characteristics of the action.

살다 = to live
사 + -ㄴ다는 것 → 산다는 것 = the act of living, life
외국에 산다는 것은 가끔 힘들 때도 있어요. = The nature of living overseas is that there are sometimes hard times.

Sometimes, -(ㄴ/는)다는 것 can be combined with a particle and shortened to -(느/는)다는 건 (combined with -은) or -(느/는)다는 게 (-이), which often happens in spoken language for easier pronunciation.

Ex)
하다 → 한다는 것이 = 한다는 게
하다 → 한다는 것은 = 한다는 건

Sample Sentences

혼자 공부한다는 것은 생각만큼 쉽지 않아요.

= Studying alone is not as easy as you think.

> * You could say, "혼자 공부하는 것은 생각만큼 쉽지 않아요" but by saying "혼자 공부한다는 것은…", you are talking about the general nature of studying alone rather than just talking about yourself when you study alone.

주말에도 회사에 가야 한다는 건 정말 슬픈 일이에요.

= Having to go to work on the weekend is so sad.

아이를 키운다는 건 참 힘든 일이에요.

= Raising a child is very tough.

Track 55

한국에서 유명한 가수가 된다는 건 정말 어려운 일이에요.

= Becoming a famous singer in Korea is a very difficult thing.

장학금을 받는다는 것은 정말 대단한 일이에요.

= Receiving a scholarship is (an) amazing (achievement).

Sample Dialogue

경화: 이 영화는 제가 정말 좋아하는 영화예요.

석진: 어떤 내용인데요?

경화: '아버지가 된다는 것은 무엇일까?'라고 물어보는 영화예요.

석진: 오! 재밌을 것 같네요. 요즘 가족이 된다는 것이 어떤 의미인지에 대해서 이야기하는 영화가 많은 것 같아요.

Kyung-hwa: This movie is one that I really like.

Seokjin: What is it about?

Kyung-hwa: It's a movie that asks, "I wonder what it means to become a father."

Seokjin: Oh, that sounds fun. It seems like there are a lot of movies that talk about what becoming a family means these days.

✏ *Exercises for Lesson* **28**

Replace -**는 것** *with* -*(ㄴ/는)***다는 것** *in order to imply that you are talking about the nature/ characteristics of an action.*

1. 배우는 것은 언제나 즐거운 일이에요.

....

2. 혼자 공부하는 것은 생각만큼 쉽지 않아요.

....

3. 아이를 키우는 것은 참 힘든 일이에요.

....

4. 외국에 사는 것은 가끔 힘들 때도 있어요.

....

5. 한국에서 유명한 가수가 되는 것은 정말 어려운 일이에요.

....

Check the answers on **P.203**

LESSON 29

So that..., To the point where...

-도록

Track 57

In this lesson, let us take a look at the verb ending -도록, which means "so that", "in a way that" or sometimes "to the point where" in Korean.

-도록 has three main usages:

1. The verb before -도록 can express the objective of the following verb.

2. The verb before -도록 can express the effect or the method leading to the following verb.

3. The verb before -도록 can express the extent or degree of the following state or action.

Usages

1. Expressing the objective of the following verb

    Ex)

지나가다 = to pass through

→ 지나가도록

Tell Stories, Express Ideas, and

사람들이 지나가도록 비켜 주세요.

= Please step aside so that people can pass through.

이해하다 = to understand

→ 이해할 수 있도록

제가 이해할 수 있도록 설명해 주세요.

= Please explain so that I can understand.

2. Expressing the effect or the method leading to the following verb

Ex)

들리다 = to be heard

→ 들리도록.

Track 57

다 들리도록 이야기해 주세요.

= Please talk in a way so that everyone can hear you.

= Please talk so that everyone can hear you.

볼 수 있다 = to be able to see

→ 볼 수 있도록

제가 볼 수 있도록 놓아 주세요.

= Please put it in a way that I can see it.

3. Expressing the extent or degree of the following state or action

Ex)

아프다 = to be painful

→ 아프도록

목이 아프도록 노래를 불렀어요.

= I sang a lot, to the point where my throat hurt.

질리다 = to get sick of, to get tired of

→ 질리도록

바나나를 질리도록 먹었어요.

= I ate so many bananas that I got sick of them.

Track 57

* Usages 1 and 2 overlap in some contexts and Usages 2 and 3 also overlap in some contexts.

Sample Sentences

그 얘기는 귀가 아프도록 많이 들었어요.

= I heard that story so often, almost to the point of my ears hurting.

늦지 않도록* 빨리 서두르세요.

= Hurry up so that you will not be late.

    * Here you have a negative form with -도록. You can use -도록 with negative forms.

    Also, when you use -도록 after 않, it sounds like [안토록].

넘어지지 않도록 주의해 주세요.

= Please be careful so that you do not fall over.

제가 이해하기 쉽도록 설명했어요.

= I explained it in a way that would be easy to understand.

이 신발은 다 떨어지도록 자주 신었어요.

= I have worn these shoes so often, almost to the point where they are worn out.

Track 57

Sample Dialogue

Track 58

주연: 요즘 잠을 못 자서 너무 피곤해요.

석진: 왜 잠을 못 잤어요?

주연: 매일 밤늦도록 일하느라고요.

석진: 힘내요. 내일 주말이잖아요.
　　　주말에 질리도록 자요.

Jooyeon: I'm so tired because I can't sleep these days.

Seokjin: Why couldn't you sleep?

Jooyeon: Because I was working late into the night every day.

Seokjin: Cheer up. Tomorrow is the weekend, isn't it? Sleep to the point where you get sick of sleeping on the weekend.

Tell Stories, Express Ideas, and

✎ Exercises for Lesson 29

Fill in the blanks by using -도록.

Check the answers on **p.203**

1. 사람들이 (   ) 비켜 주세요.

  = Please step aside so that people can pass through.

2. 바나나를 (   ) 먹었어요.

  = I ate so many bananas that I got sick of them.

3. 목이 (   ) 노래를 불렀어요.

  = I sang a lot, to the point where my throat hurt.

4. 다 (   ) 이야기해 주세요.

  = Please talk in a way so that everyone can hear you.

  = Please talk so that everyone can hear you.

5. 제가 (   ) 설명해 주세요.

  = Please explain so that I can understand.

LESSON **30**

Sentence Building Drill 11

Sentence Building Drill 11

Track 59

In this series, we focus on how you can use the grammatical rules and expressions that you have learned so far to train yourself to comfortably and flexibly make more Korean sentences.

We will start off with THREE key sentences, then practice changing parts of these sentences so that you do not end up just memorizing the same three sentences. We want you to be able to be as flexible as possible with the Korean sentences that you can make.

Key Sentence (1)

다른 사람들한테 물어보나 마나, 제가 맞다고 할 거예요.

= Even if you ask other people, they will say I am right.

Key Sentence (2)

이건 계속 연습하기만 하면 잘하게 되어 있어요.

= As long as you keep practicing this, you are bound to get better at it.

Key Sentence (3)

여기는 날씨도 추운 데다가, 물가도 비싼 편이에요.

= On top of being cold here, the prices are rather high, too.

Expansion & Variation Practice with Key Sentence (1)

0. Original Sentence:

다른 사람들한테 물어보나 마나, 제가 맞다고 할 거예요.

= Even if you ask other people, they will say I am right.

1.

다른 사람들한테 물어보나 마나 = (Regardless of) Whether you ask other people or not...

확인해 보나 마나 = (Regardless of) Whether you check or not...

거기까지 가나 마나 = (Regardless of) Whether you go all the way there or not...

열심히 하나 마나 = (Regardless of) Whether you work hard on it or not...

사진을 많이 찍으나 마나 = (Regardless of) Whether you take a lot of photos or not...

Track
59

2.

제가 맞다고 할 거예요. = They will say that I am right.

이게 제일 좋다고 했어요. = They said that this is the best one.

어렵지 않다고 했어요. = They said that it is not difficult.

혼자 간다고 했어요. = He said that he would go there alone.

바쁘다고 할 거예요. = They will say that they are busy.

Expansion & Variation Practice with Key Sentence (2)

0. Original Sentence:

이건 계속 연습하기만 하면 잘하게 되어 있어요.

= As long as you keep practicing this, you are bound to get better at it.

1.

이건 계속 연습하기만 하면 = As long as you keep practicing this...

중간에 그만두지만 않으면 = As long as you do not quit in the middle...

사람들이 계속 봐 주기만 하면 = As long as people keep watching it...

손님이 계속 오기만 하면 = As long as customers keep coming...

멀리 가지만 않으면 = As long as you do not go far...

Track 59

2.

잘하게 되어 있어요. = You are bound to get better at it.

사람들이 알게 되어 있어요. = People will surely find out eventually.

다시 만나게 되어 있어요. = You are bound to meet again.

돌아오게 되어 있어요. = They will come back for sure.

해결되게 되어 있어요. = It is bound to be solved.

Expansion & Variation Practice with Key Sentence (3)

0. Original Sentence:

여기는 날씨도 추운 데다가, 물가도 비싼 편이에요.

= On top of being cold here, the prices are rather high, too.

I.

여기는 날씨도 추운 데다가 = On top of being cold, this place...

요즘 시간도 없는 데다가 = These days, on top of having no time...

아직 숙제를 다 못 한 데다가 = I have not finished all my homework yet, and on top of that...

어제 늦게 잠든 데다가 = I went to sleep late yesterday, and in addition to that...

영어를 잘하는 데다가 = On top of speaking English well...

2.

물가도 비싼 편이에요. = The prices are rather high, too.

키도 큰 편이에요. = He is also quite tall.

분위기도 좋은 편이에요. = The atmosphere is also pretty nice.

일도 잘하는 편이에요. = He is quite good at what he does, too.

중국어도 잘하는 편이에요. = She speaks fairly good Chinese as well.

Track 59

Sample Dialogue

주연: 내일 아침 비행기는 보나 마나 결항될
　　　것 같아요.

경화: 아니에요. 바람이 많이 불지만 않으면
　　　비행기 뜰 수 있대요.

주연: 아, 정말요?

경화: 네. 그래서 비 오는 날보다 바람 많이
　　　부는 날 결항이 더 자주 되는 편이에요.

*Jooyeon: I think flights for tomorrow morning will
be canceled without a doubt.*

*Kyung-hwa: No they won't. As long as it isn't too
windy, I heard that planes can take off.*

Jooyeon: Oh, really?

*Kyung-hwa: Yes. Therefore, flights get canceled
more often on a windy day than on a
rainy day.*

Tell Stories, Express Ideas, and

✎ Exercises for Lesson **30**

Check the answers on **p.203**

Translate each phrase or sentence into Korean and write it on the lines provided. The subjects are in parentheses because you do not need to translate them.

1. (They) said that it is not difficult.

....

2. As long as you do not quit in the middle...

....

3. On top of speaking English well...

....

4. (You) are bound to meet again.

....

5. (She) speaks fairly good Chinese, as well.

....

BLOG

Lotus Flower Tea, Lotus Leaf Tea
(연꽃차, 연잎차)

I am sure you have heard of lotus flowers. They can be pink or white and grow in water. Around June and July, these gorgeous flowers begin to bloom. Korea does a fantastic job of creating festivals for everyone to enjoy the flowers when they bloom. If you can visit Korea during this time of the year, I highly recommend it.

Along with lotus flowers being beautiful to look at, they can also be quite tasty. Well, maybe not the leaf itself, as it can be a bit bitter tasting. I know, because I was told to try one once. However, I kind of liked the taste. My friend who was with me on the other hand, did not quite like it. But I am not here to tell you about the taste of the actual leaf, but about the tea you can make from it. That is right, you can make lotus flower/leaf tea.

The first time I ever tried it was about a year ago. Before this, I had no idea you could make tea from it. I was invited to a café that specialized in lotus tea in the south of Seoul. I had no idea what to expect, and when it came out, I was completely blown away. They brought out this ceramic bowl filled with water and a white lotus flower was floating in the center.

After letting it sit for a short time, you take a ladle, dip it into the bowl, and pour the tea into your cup. It tastes sweet but is not too strong, which surprised me since the petal that I took a bite out of earlier was so bitter. On a hot day, the tea was very soothing and surprisingly very delicious. While drinking the tea, we were also given some cookies that were made

195

from a lotus flower and boy were they good! We ended up taking a box home, but I am not sure they made it more than two days.

Flash forward a year and my wife and I were curious if there was anything like this on Jeju. Since we moved here a little over a year ago, we are always trying to find cool spots to visit and take our friends. We found a place that was not too far from our house so decided to drive over to it.

When we first got to the café, we weren't sure if it was open or not. We found the door we thought we were supposed to enter and opened it. No one was around so we decided to call out and see if we were allowed to enter. The owner replied and told us to come in and make ourselves comfortable. The café only had a couple of tables and had a gallery of the owner's artwork. She sells her art which mainly uses lotus flowers; it was all quite beautiful.

The café owner even used some of the dried lotus flowers in her artwork; I think my wife wants to try that now, too! Behind the café was a small garden which was the perfect spot to spend a couple of hours on a cool day. After exploring the café and looking at all of the artwork, we sat down with the owner and began drinking our tea.

She brought out two bowls instead of one like the first place. In one bowl was the lotus flower, and in the other bowl was the green leaf that typically floats with the lotus flower. We tried the one with the lotus flower first, and it had a very similar taste to the tea that I tried the first time. She then told us that the one with the green leaf was a bit stronger so we tried it next. It was indeed a stronger taste but still not overbearing. She then told us to mix the two types as they blend together perfectly since one is sweet and one is bitter. Depending on which one you like more, you can opt to add more from one or the other to suit your taste.

We sat there with the owner talking about life, tea, and her artwork. It was a wonderful time that my wife and I will certainly never forget. We must have been really enjoying ourselves because before we knew it, it was already dinner time. We spent several hours listening to stories which is the best way to enjoy lotus leaf tea.

Once we were ready to leave (we also did not want to take up any more of the owner's time), she gave us the leaves and told us we could continue drinking it at home. Then, once we finished drinking it, we could let the flowers dry and use it to decorate our house. For the price, I say it was certainly worth it. Not only did we have some great company, we had some amazing tea and we got to take something home with us to use as decoration.

Written by Johnny Bland

ANSWERS
for Level 7, Lessons 1 ~ 30

Answers for Level 7, Lesson 1

1.

(존댓말) 여기 있었군요.

(반말) 여기 있었구나.

= (I see that) It was here.

2.

(존댓말) 생각보다 비싸군요.

(반말) 생각보다 비싸구나.

= (I see that) It is more expensive than I thought.

3.

(존댓말) 여기 사는군요.

(반말) 여기 사는구나.

= (I see that) You live here.

4.

(존댓말) 이렇게 하는 거군요.

(반말) 이렇게 하는 거구나.

= So this is how you do it!

5.

(존댓말) 이게 그거였군요.

(반말) 이게 그거였구나.

= So this was about what you were talking!

Answers for Level 7, Lesson 2

1. 아는 척하다 or 아는 체하다

2. 자는 척하다 or 자는 체하다

3. 자고 있는 척하다 or 자고 있는 체하다

4. 예쁜 척하다 or 예쁜 체하다

5. 일하고 있는 척하다 or 일하고 있는 체하다

Answers for Level 7, Lesson 3

1. 그럴 만해요

2. 있을 만해요 or 많을 만해요

3. 읽을 만해요

4. 참을 만해요

5. 갈 만해요 or 방문할 만해요

Answers for Level 7, Lesson 4

1. 저 같은 사람 처음 봤어요? = Did you see a person like me for the first time?

2. 저 사람이랑 같이 하세요. = Do it together with that person.

3. 그 사람은 한국어를 한국 사람같이 잘해요. = He/She speaks Korean well like a Korean person.

4. 바보같이 정말 그 말을 믿었어요? = Did you really believe that like a fool?

5. 오늘은 일요일 같은 월요일이에요. = Today is a Monday (that feels) like a Sunday.

Answers for Level 7, Lesson 5

1. 필요한 만큼

2. 먹을 만큼만

3. 한국에서만큼

4. 경화 씨만큼

5. 얼마만큼

Answers for Level 7, Lesson 6

1. 원 (院)

2. 대학원 (大學院)

3. 병원 (病院)

4. 입원 (入院)

199

5. 법원 (法院)

Answers for Level 7, Lesson 7

1. 울어 봤자

2. 모르는 척해 봤자

3. 있어 봤자

4. 말해 봤자

5. 출발해 봤자 or 가 봤자

Answers for Level 7, Lesson 8

1. 했길래

2. 가길래

3. 올 것 같길래

4. 있길래

5. 많길래

Answers for Level 7, Lesson 9

1. 하느라고

2. 일하느라고

3. 내느라고

4. 운동하느라고

Answers for Level 7, Lesson 10

1. 제가 말한 것처럼

2. 그냥 바쁜 척했어요.

3. 집에 우유가 없길래

4. 아무리 걱정해 봤자 소용없어요.

5. 아무리 서둘러 봤자 이미 늦었어요.

Answers for Level 7, Lesson 11

1. 좁히다 = to make something narrower

2. 낮추다 = to lower, to make something lower

3. 울리다 = to make someone cry

4. 신기다 = to make someone wear (shoes/socks)

5. 넘기다 = to make something go over something

6. 재우다 = to make someone sleep

7. 밝히다 = to brighten

8. 높이다 = to make something higher, to heighten

9. 넓히다 = to widen

10. 키우다 = to make something bigger, to grow

Answers for Level 7, Lesson 12

1. 그 영화 어제 봤는데, 재미있더라. = I saw that movie yesterday, and it was fun.

2. 어제 경화 씨 만났는데, 머리를 염색했더라. = I met Kyung-hwa yesterday, and she had dyed her hair.

3. 싱가포르에 처음 가 봤는데, 정말 덥더라. = I went to Singapore for the first time, and it was really hot there.

4. 윤아 씨한테 물어봤는데, 모르더라. = I asked Yoona, and she did not know.

5. 아까 주연 씨 만났는데, 친구랑 있더라. = I met Jooyeon earlier, and she was with her friend.

Answers for Level 7, Lesson 13

1. 기 (機)

2. 자판기 (自販機)

3. 비행기 (飛行機)

4. 계산기 (計算機)

5. 복사기 (複寫機)

Answers for Level 7, Lesson 14

1. 아무리 맛있어도

2. 아무리 싫어도

3. 아무리 바빠도

4. 아무리 비싸도

5. 아무리 늦어도

Answers for Level 7, Lesson 15

1. 이거 누구 거였지? = Whose is this? (I forgot.)

2. 그 사람 이름이 뭐였지? = What was his name again?

3. 주연 씨 생일이 언제였지? = When was Jooyeon's birthday again? / When is Jooyeon's birthday? (I forgot.)

4. 이거 누구 책이었지? = Whose book was this again? / (I forgot,) Whose book is this?

5. 이게 한국어로 뭐였지? = What was this in Korean again?

Answers for Level 7, Lesson 16

1. 모른다니까요. = I said I do not know.

2. 바쁘다니까요. = I said I am busy.

3. 혼자 갈 거라니까요. = I said I am going alone!

4. 제가 안 했다니까요. = I said I did not do it!

5. 저는 정말 몰랐다니까요. = I said I really did not know.

Answers for Level 7, Lesson 17

1. 이게 제일 좋대요. = They say that this is the best.

2. 벌써 다 끝났대요. = They say it has ended already.

3. 제 친구가 한국에 올 거래요. = I hear that my friend will come to Korea.

4. 이 사람 정말 유명한 사람이래요. = They say this person is a very famous person.

5. 그 사람은 한국에 와 본 적이 없대요. = They say he has never come to Korea.

Answers for Level 7, Lesson 18

1. 지금 온다던데요. = She says she is coming now. (+ So should we wait? / What do you think?)

2. 그 사람 유명하다던데요. = They say he is famous. (+ But you said otherwise, right?)

3. 그 사람 학생이라던데요. = He says he is a student. (+ What shall we do then?)

4. 여기 위험하다던데요. = I heard that this place is dangerous. (+ What do you think?)

5. 벌써 다 끝났다던데요. = They said that it was already all over. (+ There was nothing I could do.)

Answers for Level 7, Lesson 19

1. 몇 시에 올 거냐고 물어보세요. = Ask him what time he will come here.

2. 학생이냐고 물어봤어요. = They asked me if I was a student. / I asked her if she was a student.

3. 몇 살이냐고 물어봤어요. = (Someone) asked me how old I was.

4. 저한테 어디 가냐고 말했어요. = He asked me where I was going. ("저한테 어디 가냐고 물어봤어요." is also possible.)

5. 저도 가야 되냐고 물어봐 주세요. = Please ask them if I have to come along, too.

Answers for Level 7, Lesson 20

1. 아무리 어려워도

2. 영화 본 다음에

3. 지금 자면 안 돼요.

4. 오늘 서울은 날씨가 춥대요.

5. 생각보다 어렵더라고요.

Answers for Level 7, Lesson 21

1. 싫다잖아요 or 싫어한다잖아요

2. 바쁘다잖아요

3. 실수였다잖아요

4. 아니라잖아요 or 사실이 아니라잖아요

5. 맞다잖아요 or 진짜라잖아요

Answers for Level 7, Lesson 22

1. 정 (定)

2. 결정 (決定)

3. 정가 (定價)

4. 고정 (固定)

5. 예정 (豫定)

Answers for Level 7, Lesson 23

1. 물어보나 마나

2. 하나 마나

3. 이야기를 하나 마나 or 이야기하나 마나

4. 보나 마나

5. 읽으나 마나

Answers for Level 7, Lesson 24

1.
잡다
잡히다
잡혀 있다

2.
깨다
깨지다
깨져 있다

3.
켜다
켜지다
켜져 있다

4.
쌓다
쌓이다
쌓여 있다

5.
열다
열리다
열려 있다

Answers for Level 7, Lesson 25

1. 사람들이 알게 되어 있어요

2. 열심히 하게 되어 있어요

3. 좋아지게 되어 있어요 or 오르게 되어 있어요

4. 생기게 되어 있어요

5. 집 청소를 하게 되어 있어요 or 집을 청소하게 되어

있어요

Answers for Level 7, Lesson 26

1. 잘생긴 데다가

2. 똑똑한 데다가

3. 예쁜 데다가

4. 시끄러운 데다가

5. 많은 데다가

Answers for Level 7, Lesson 27

1. 비밀을 지키는 한 안전해요.

2. 깨지지 않는 한, 계속 쓸 수 있어요.

3. 여기에 있는 한 괜찮아요.

4. 사람들이 너무 많이 오지 않는 한 괜찮아요.

5. 너무 춥지 않는 한 갈게요.

Answers for Level 7, Lesson 28

1. 배운다는 것은 언제나 즐거운 일이에요.

2. 혼자 공부한다는 것은 생각만큼 쉽지 않아요.

3. 아이를 키운다는 것은 참 힘든 일이에요.

4. 외국에 산다는 것은 가끔 힘들 때도 있어요.

5. 한국에서 유명한 가수가 된다는 것은 정말 어려운 일이
에요.

*You can always shorten 것은 to 건.

Answers for Level 7, Lesson 29

1. 지나가도록

2. 질리도록

3. 아프도록

4. 들리도록

5. 이해할 수 있도록

Answers for Level 7, Lesson 30

1. 어렵지 않다고 했어요.

2. 중간에 그만두지만 않으면

3. 영어를 잘하는 데다가

4. 다시 만나게 되어 있어요.

5. 중국어도 잘하는 편이에요.

MP3 audio files can be downloaded at http://TalkToMeInKorean.com/audio.